THE ROAD AHEAD

A VISION FOR SPIRITUAL LEADERSHIP IN THE 21ST CENTURY

JERE D. PATZER

D. Min., M.B.A.

Pacific Press® Publishing Association
Nampa, Idaho
Oshawa, Ontario, Canada
PacificPress.com

Copyright © 2003 by
Pacific Press® Publishing Association
Printed in United States of America
All Rights Reserved

Additional copies of this book may be purchased at
http://www.adventistbookcenter.com

Library of Congress Cataloging-in-Publication Data

Patzer, Jere.
The road ahead: a vision for spiritual leadership in the 21st century/Jere D. Patzer.
p. cm.
ISBN: 0-8163-1972-3
1. Christian leadership—Seventh-day Adventists. I. Title.
BV652.1 .P385 2003
262'.146732—dc21   2002192468

03 04 05 06 07 • 5 4 3 2 1

DEDICATION

This book is dedicated to the many great leaders of this church—some of whom I have had the distinct privilege of working with closely.

And especially to:

Bruce Johnston, an inspired spiritual leader
with a global view of mission.

Max Torkelsen, Sr., a visionary and transparent communicator.

Don Reynolds, a disciplined, cutting-edge mentor.

Pearl and A. J. Patzer, a steady, indefatigable,
and totally dedicated parental team.

Bryce Pascoe, a wise counselor and trusted confidant.

Cindy Stewart, a loyal servant-leader and career
executive assistant.

Darin and Troy Patzer, symbols of the new generation of creative, talented, and committed professional church leaders.

Reaction to
The Road Ahead

"Our ability to appreciate, perceive, and benefit from the future is enhanced by an appreciation for, and a good understanding of the past. Patzer looks forward, but without losing sight of the old standards and the changeless principles, that have been crucial in making us what we are. He is not a captive of the future, because he remains grounded in the Word and loyal to the Church. His book is a mirror of his own leadership, and he presents his position with boldness and conviction. Here is a good place to start if you are interested in church leadership."

HAROLD W. BAPTISTE

General vice-president, General Conference of Seventh-day Adventists

"Patzer is recognized as one of the top leaders in our Church. In this book he combines the skillful management techniques with spiritual leadership dynamics that have made him and other leaders successful."

DON SCHNEIDER

President, North American Division of Seventh-day Adventists

"In this book, Dr. Jere Patzer brings passion and energy to the task of addressing contemporary challenges that confront the Seventh-day Adventist Church. Colorful, concrete, and well illustrated, the book . . . is interesting and readable, providing insights into issues denominational leaders face in managing the mission of a conservative church in a modern world."

DONALD R. AMMON
President & CEO, Adventist Health System/West

"I would encourage every pastor and church leader—in fact, every church member—to read *The Road Ahead*. Dr. Patzer has not only outlined with clarity the challenges facing God's church in the twenty-first century, he has provided insights into how we can effectively cooperate with the Spirit to move the church forward as we grow ourselves spiritually and professionally. I personally incorporate many of these principles into my own life and work for God."

BOB KYTE
President, Pacific Press Publishing Association.

"I sense a resonance within you that I share for an unapologetic stance squarely in the heart of Adventism's raison d'etre. We are a radical, prophetic community that has been raised up by God to champion the truth about His relentless love and urgent preoccupation in arousing the attention of this lost civilization. That we are so easily dissuaded or distracted from that message only proves the critical necessity of a laser-beam focus on the mission and the message."

DWIGHT K. NELSON
Senior Pastor, Pioneer Memorial Church

CONTENTS

FOREWORD

You've heard about the lay leader who in introducing the new pastor to the church said, "He is someone who can lead this church into the twentieth century." Someone seated on the platform whispered, "You mean the twenty-first century." To which the lay leader replied, "No, as out of touch as this church is, I'd be glad to get it into the twentieth century!"

As Adventist leaders we have the challenge of *leading* our organization in a fast changing environment, not merely reacting to that transition. Additionally, we have a heritage and a mission to which we must always be true.

When I am driving my car down the road, I had better be focused on what lies ahead. However, I also must occasionally check the rear view mirror to see where I've been.

As leaders we've been told that we can have confidence for the future only as we do not forget how God has led us in our past history (see Ellen G. White, *Selected Messages,* book 3, p. 162). I'd suggest that we can likewise maintain our focus and our direction only as we recall from whence we've come.

It is increasingly easy for a multiethnic, multicultural, multigenerational, multilinguistic church to have so many programs that the fundamental focus of God's church can be lost. There are good things that can sap our energy and resources yet not contribute to the direct accomplishment of the mission of this church. Sharing the good news of Jesus Christ in the unique context of the great controversy is still the only rationale for the existence of the prophetic remnant church.

As someone said, "That's where the rubber meets . . . the sky"; with a glance over our shoulder to guarantee our continuation on the right track, yet moving ahead toward a climactic heavenly conclusion.

We have not been called merely to be managers. We have been called to leadership. Managers manage programs. Leaders lead people.

As a leader reading this book, may you recommit to the heritage that brought us to where we are today, and at the same time may you be challenged to become a more effective leader, a change agent moving your organization forward through the people you lead.

"The art of progress is to preserve order amid change and to preserve change amid order."
—*Alfred North Whitehead.*

"Christ raised up this prophetic church by inspiring its theology, which drives its mission, made possible by its organization."
—*Jere D. Patzer.*

CHAPTER 1

THE CHURCH WE LEAD

The biblical account has never been more accurate than when it says, "The devil walks about like a roaring lion, seeking whom he may devour" (1 Peter 5:8, NKJV). In fact I recently noted with dismay the words of Ellen White who says, "The power of Satan now to tempt and deceive is ten-fold greater than it was in the days of the apostles" (*Spiritual Gifts,* vol. 2, p. 277).

Confirming Daniel's prophecy regarding the increase in end-time knowledge, Robert Tuttle, former CEO of the billion-dollar SPX Corporation, has said that man's cumulative knowledge has doubled in the last decade and will double again every five years. Bill Gates, founder of Microsoft, says that business is going to change more in the next ten years than it has in the last fifty.

RADICAL CHANGE IS AFFECTING THE WORLD AND THE CHURCH

We live in a time of radical change. And if there are radical changes taking place in the business world, it is only logical that the same thing is happening within the church. The Seventh-day

Adventist Church has been featured prominently in a major book by a top American scholar, William S. Bainbridge. Thankfully, he was very gracious to us. He states that Seventh-day Adventists "have taken their place among major denominations." Then he goes on with this interesting perspective: "Like other conservative denominations, the SDA Church has struggled to preserve its traditional beliefs and practices while confronting the challenges of a rapidly changing world" (*The Sociology of Religious Movement*, pp. 107, 108).

So dynamic change is taking place in our world and in our church. And as church thought leaders, we must realize that we need to have a whole new way of thinking in order to meet these changes. If being aware of change is of number one importance, then responding to it must be the logical next step. Meanwhile, the authority and integrity of the organization are being challenged from within, and theological counterfeits and aberrations are multiplying.

TIMELY RESPONSE IS IMPERATIVE

Vision, mission, focus, and commitment for the future have almost become cliches. Management authors, Tom Peters and Robert H. Waterman, Jr., talk about "ready, fire, aim." It's one thing to have commitment and vision, but it's something else to act upon them in a timely way. As I recall, the famous hockey player, Wayne Gretzsky, once said, "I don't skate to where the puck is. I skate to where it's going to be." In the biblical setting, Noah didn't build his ark in the rain.

Lee Iaccoca of Chrysler fame is a classic example of a modern-day visionary. He not only dreamed, but also acted on his dreams. A few years ago Iaccoca asked one of his engineers, "Do you think a convertible will sell again?"

The engineer's response was, "It will take three years to design one."

Iaccoca retorted, "No! Saw off the top of a car and give me one this afternoon!" As he drove around town, he counted the hands of smiling people waving and pointing. The very next year Chrysler had a new convertible model on the market.

The challenges of today demand a timely responsiveness like never before in history. As church members, you and I had better be prepared—despite the complexity and difficulty—to respond to the changes taking place in our church.

FACE THE FUTURE WHILE REMEMBERING OUR PAST

The road in the twenty-first century seems to come at us as fast as does the road that the kids face in those video arcade car races. We need to look ahead through the windshield to avoid every possible obstacle and pothole. At the same time we must keep one eye on the mirror, mindful of whence we've come. Sayings such as "Back to the future," "Try it again for the first time" should be more than mere slick advertising slogans.

We have a tremendous heritage of which we are rightfully proud. Let's not be afraid of going back to the basics.

I can never forget the classic line from the famous Green Bay Packers coach, Vince Lombardi, as he stood before his football team, hoping to motivate them by emphasizing the basics. "Gentlemen," he said, "This is a football." He taught his players superlative execution in the context of basic fundamentals.

So let's review the very bedrock principles for the framework of the church we lead. And in that context I would like to suggest a very basic premise. It's easily illustrated by an equilateral triangle.

MY THESIS

My basic premise in this book is simply this: *I believe God raised up our prophetic church by inspiring its theology, which drives its mission, made possible by its organization.* In graphic terms, it looks like this:

Seventh-day Adventist Church

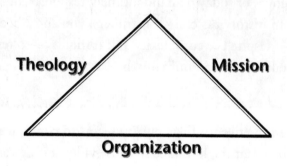

All three of these elements are intrinsically linked. All three are divinely ordained. All three are profoundly significant. Diminishing any part will cause the whole to collapse or possibly implode with drastic consequences.

Let me defend that thesis.

OUR HISTORIC THEOLOGY

Our Protestant heritage gave us an inspired and corrected view of inspiration and revelation. This view was not complex or hard to understand.

To adapt the words of Vince Lombardi, *"Ladies and gentlemen, this is a Bible."* This is God's inspired Word. It doesn't merely contain His Word to be evaluated, critiqued, dissected, or adapted because of scientific or archeological data—no matter how plausible, intellectually stimulating, or ego gratifying that may appear to be. As Christians, we must always allow the Bible to inform our understanding of science and archaeology.

Neither Christ nor His disciples spent time pointing out the supposed inconsistencies of the Scriptures, including the Genesis accounts of Creation and the Flood. Rather, Christ commended the writings of Moses to His listeners (see Luke 16:29). If the Bible could specifically predict, in minute detail, the events surrounding the birth and life of Jesus, couldn't it record with specificity and accuracy the early history of the earth?

If Paul were writing to us today rather than to Timothy, I believe he'd say, "All Scripture is given by inspiration . . . and I still mean *all*" (adapted from 2 Timothy 3:16).

I once heard two thought leaders quoted on the radio. The first was Dr. Billy Graham, who said, "I have no problem with the fish swallowing Jonah. If the Bible said that Jonah swallowed the fish, I would have believed it!" And mystic A. W. Tozier said, "Give me Genesis 1:1, 'In the beginning God ...' and the rest of the Bible gives me no problem."

I realize that there are those that would look pejoratively on such attitudes and quickly label them as "too fundamentalist." They would contrast this kind of attitude with being led by the Holy Spirit, which to them seems to allow for more freedom.

A recent quote in the *Washington Post* by Michael Morse, a United Church of Christ minister, helps put this contrast in perspective and demonstrates a possible, if not natural, outgrowth of this false dichotomy:

> For some Christians, the Bible is always authoritative. They are called fundamentalists. For others, however, Jesus Christ is authoritative. To treat the Bible literally leads to all

kinds of serious distortions and cruelties. To treat Jesus seriously leads one to the inevitable conclusion that He believed in lifestyles filled with equality, mutuality, compassion, commitment, responsibility, and love. There is plenty of room in those lifestyles for gay persons, even for gay marriages (quoted in *First Things First,* March 1997, p. 62).

Being led by the Holy Spirit and adhering to the authority of Scripture are, however, never mutually exclusive.

Furthermore when we need additional amplification, I know where we can find it. Most of us have a shelf full of those special old books that need to be dusted off and used again. Admittedly in the past they have been abused and misused. *But now they are unused—or as the author herself predicted—made "of none effect."* (see *Selected Messages,* bk. 3, p. 73).

Why should the messenger of the Lord be ignored? Why should we be ashamed of her and her ministry? Certainly there are other denominations that have much less to offer with their prophets. Yet they promote them. Why would we rather base our beliefs on some little-known scientist, archaeologist, or psychologist whose theories change with each new discovery, when we have God's messenger who, if my understanding is correct, is:

- The fourth most translated author in the history of literature.
- The most translated woman writer in the history of the world.
- The most translated American author, male or female.

Recently I spoke to a large group of health-care administrators and mentioned that I was not embarrassed by the fact that while getting a doctorate in church administration and an MBA in management, I got some of those old books down from the shelf, dusted them off, and read them from cover to cover—the Bible, the *Conflict of the Ages* series, the nine-volume *Testimonies for the Church,* and the E. G. White biographies. I had to do that because of my personal need to go back to the basics. I wanted to familiarize myself again with the truths they contain, and subconsciously, if need be, undergird my personalized, fundamental *modus operandi* of management. I wanted these books to be more than just nice devotional works. And I can testify that they are still relevant and dynamic in the twenty-first century.

Certainly the times have changed. Names and cities and people are different. But the core issues and the basic principles are identical. How can we somehow forget or fail to understand that the God who inspired the great visionary Ellen White with the knowledge to start our health-care institutions, our educational institutions, or our church will also provide us with sufficient knowledge for their current and future success? It was He who asked us— commanded us, actually—to be the head, not the tail. And He has also reminded us that those of this world are sometimes wiser and more sensitive to the truth than those who are supposed to be of the light.

Within God's Word and the writings of Ellen White, I have found counsels and philosophies that will indeed make us the head—*if* we follow them. These are counsels that guarantee us success even when it appears that we are going against the most advanced or conventional human wisdom. They contain better information than any theological, archeological, psychological, or management book written.

Let's not apologize. Let's read them, endorse them, and, yes, publicly quote them.

I sincerely believe that as we get back to the Bible and the writings of Ellen White, we will find that they clearly and in a unified way predict our unique role in the challenges we face.

There are those who advocate that we should jettison the baggage of some of our unique historical doctrines. In a fierce and cunningly persuasive attack Kenneth Richard Samples states in his foreword to Dale Ratzlaff's book *The Cultic Doctrine of Seventh-day Adventists:* "Some of the distinctive Adventist beliefs that were originated by its pioneers still plague the contemporary church."

A similar challenge that has gained acceptability in some circles is the notion that Adventists can pick and choose—like some giant theological cafeteria—which doctrines are important. When questioned where he stood, one person responded, "I'm Adventist enough." But our relationship to God and to His church must be grounded more firmly than that. Our doctrines while individually defensible are unitedly inseparable. There is a golden thread that ties them together and brings harmony, symmetry, and beauty to our message. As leaders we must not let it break.

Let me give you a few illustrations. Recently, a friend stated in our Sabbath School class that we should not take the Creation account in Genesis 1 too literally. "For example," he stated, "if we accept the Creation story as it reads, the sun wasn't created until the fourth day. Yet the Bible says 'the evening and the morning were the first day' [Genesis 1:5]. But there couldn't have been an evening and a morning on that first day without the sun."

Now I'm not a scientist, and I realize that creationists face challenges for which they don't have answers. Furthermore, I respect the fact that we have scholars willing to wrestle with issues that most of us church leaders don't regularly contend with. However, there are significant consequences to our entire belief system if we begin to allow our science to inform our theology rather than our theology to inform our science. The Bible must always be the higher authority since it is "impossible for God to lie" (Hebrews 6:18). And the facts are that if we get away from the twenty-four-hour, seven-consecutive-day Creation, we definitely lose the significance of a weekly seventh-day Sabbath.

I don't have an answer for how there could be an evening and morning before the creation of the sun. But if I have enough faith to believe that God created a world, then it makes sense to me that if He wanted to start a sequence of darkness and light before there was a sun, He could figure that out too. In fact, God may have wanted to say symbolically to later generations, "I want you to worship the Creator Son not the later-created sun." So however He did it, I suspect that this is just one of a whole series of questions He'll answer for us throughout eternity.

Some Adventists deride belief in a universal flood as impossible. Nevertheless let me share with you just two of the many reasons why I believe it happened. First, the Bible says it. Second, if God were talking only about a local flood, then any time there is a rainbow it would make God a liar because that is His sign that there will never be another worldwide flood. Localized floods don't qualify.

So if there's no universal flood, then we have a problem with the geologic column—we have the specter of death happening before sin is recorded. If that's true, then we have a problem with substitutionary atonement, and certainly we have a problem with the literal twenty-four-hour, seven-day Creation account given in the Bible.

Today there are those who advocate a conditional eschatology—minimizing, if not eliminating, the threat of Sunday laws. They propose that the Sabbath will *not* be the final test and also that the little horn of Daniel 7 has other more contemporary explanations than the Catholic Church. Incidentally, not too many years ago, some of our people applied these symbols to communism.

The facts are that anyone reading current literature such as *The Keys of This Blood* or *The Woman Rides the Beast,* or who has traveled in Catholic countries, can see the validity of Ellen White's statement in *The Great Controversy* that the Catholic Church remains unchanged. In fact, she says, "And let it be remembered, it is the boast of Rome that she never changes.... Stealthily and unsuspectedly she is strengthening her forces to further her own ends when the time shall come for her to strike" (*The Great Controversy,* p. 581).

Tongue in cheek, if I were writing headlines for the tabloids today I'd be tempted to write, *"Princess Di, Mother Teresa, Mother Mary United in Heaven. Expecting To Visit Earth in the Early Twenty-First Century."*

With this dynamic sweeping the nation it is natural that the doctrine of the remnant that gives us uniqueness and, in reality, our *raison d'être* is also downplayed. But remember that biblically, the remnant was made up, not only of individual survivors, but it also had a corporate identity, a body. The remnant had the characteristics of a survivor nation. In Revelation 12, the remnant are the commandment keepers as a group in the end time. We believe this church was raised up for a distinct role in the closing period of earth's history. If not, we might as well join the Baptists or at least the Seventh-day Baptists—right? Wrong! Not so for me. More importantly, not so for Ellen White. Listen to what she said:

Elder K ... as far as the Sabbath is concerned, he occupies the same position as the Seventh Day Baptists. Separate the Sabbath from the messages, and it loses its power; but when connected with the message of the third angel, a power attends it which convicts unbelievers and infidels, and brings them out with strength to stand, to live, grow, and flourish in the Lord (*Testimonies for the Church,* vol. 1, p. 337).

The unique thrust of the three angels' messages gives our message special power. Ellen White said it then, and I believe that's what she would say today to the independent groups networking around the world. I believe that's what she would say to their leaders who are currently deciding which of the twenty-seven fundamental beliefs are important.

Today critics and cynics abound. But if, as they charge, the remnant is too limited, if eschatology is too conditional, if evangelists are too dependent on proof texts, and if the organization is too top heavy, why should our kids, generation Xer's, and boomers support this message or be willing to die for it?

Dean Keely, a Methodist guest-lecturer at Andrews University in the fall of 1982, made this incredibly insightful comment: "The things that I have mentioned about tithing, the seventh-day Sabbath, foot washing, etc. are the things that make the Seventh-day Adventist Church unique, distinctive, and demanding. They give it its bite, its convincingness, its seriousness. Each church needs its own way of insisting that 'you have got to live up to this to be one of us.' If you strip away all the requirements, you can render the movement feeble, pallid, and ordinary overnight. So there's the answer to your question: How can the Seventh-day Adventist Church stop growing? Be like the Methodists."

I believe emphatically that the Lord gave this church its doctrines—yes, all twenty-seven—in a marvelously connected body. In his recent paper, "American Protestant History," pastor and historian Doug Johnson shows how American Protestantism faced two pivotal issues in the post–Civil War years. First, how to relate to the Germans' new approach to interpreting the Bible—a method that became known as "higher criticism." Second, how they would relate to the Darwinian theory of evolution and it religious accommodation—theistic evolution.

The acceptance of these two views—evolutionary theory and a perspective on the Bible shaped by higher criticism—became known in religious circles as "modernism." Our church rejected this modernism and thus saved itself from disaster. By accepting the philosophies of modernism, however, many other denominations began experiencing greatly diminished growth in the 1960s and significant membership losses in the decades of the 1970s to1990s. These changes were often subtle and almost imperceptible. But they happened nonetheless.

Bradley J. Longfield, in his award-winning book *The Presbyterian Controversy,* writes about the fact that, in general, mainstream churches in America are facing a crisis. The Presbyterian Church, which is seen as representative of many denominations, lost 1.2 million members from 1966 to1987. Longfield points out that while adherence to doctrinal pluralism has maintained institutional unity, it has left the churches "devoid of a clear theological voice." He further states that the Presbyterian Church, which had maintained a strong doctrinal position, opted during the 1920s and 1930s to "widen its boundaries to preserve the mission of the church to the culture" (pp. 3, 4). He summarizes the aftermath this way:

> The Presbyterian controversy raged for fourteen years over
> such issues as ordination requirements, the mission of
> Princeton Seminary, and the orthodoxy of the Board of For-

eign Missions. Though at the height of the conflict in the mid-1920's the church managed to hold together, the controversy resulted in a loosening of the church's ordination standards, the reorganization of Princeton Theological Seminary, the creation of Westminster Theological Seminary, and the eventual founding of the Presbyterian Church of America (p. 4).

I'm reminded of what Robinson Crusoe said, "If you expand the fences too far, pretty soon the goats on the inside are just as wild as the goats on the outside!" For our purposes that can refer to our theology or to our standards. One is reminded of the fact that those who fail to learn from the past are condemned to repeat it.

God didn't just arbitrarily label us the "remnant." We have become the remnant by the fact that virtually all other evangelical denominations have either embraced or are in the process of embracing these popular views. Thus, they have by default slid into modernism, postmodernism, and neo-orthodoxy. At the risk of sounding arrogant, the Seventh-day Adventist Church may soon be positioned as the only ones left to guard the precious truths of the Scriptures. Yet some forces in our church are strongly and intentionally pushing us to forsake our sacred calling and to acquiesce to the pressure for theological plurality in order to achieve the appearance of unity.

On a closely related topic, D. A. Carson in a masterful 640-page book titled *The Gagging of God,* addresses the issue of modernism/postmodernism as it relates to the increasingly popular theories of pluralism.

In the religious field, this means that few people will be offended by the multiplying new religions. No matter how wacky, no matter how flimsy their intellectual credentials, no matter how subjective and uncontrolled, no matter how blatantly self-centered, no matter how obviously their gods have been manufactured to foster human self-promotion, the media will treat them with fascination and even a degree of respect. But if any religion claims that in some measure other religions are wrong, a line has been crossed and resentment is immediately stirred up. . . . Exclusiveness is the one religious idea that cannot be tolerated. Correspondingly, proselytism is a dirty word. One cannot fail to observe a crushing irony: the gospel of relativistic tolerance is perhaps the most "evangelistic" movement in Western culture at the moment, demanding assent and brooking no rivals (pp. 32, 33).

So first, God gave us a unique, unified, and precious theology. That leads us to our second point—our church's organization.

OUR ORGANIZATION

Today the term "postdenominationalism" is gaining credence. At the October 4, 1997, Promise Keepers Rally in Washington D.C., nearly a million men cheered as best-selling author Max Lucado proclaimed sectarianism a sin. You may have noted the following wire release from Columbus, Ohio, July 6, 1997:

The United Church of Christ decided to unite with three other Protestant denominations, sharing congregations and ministers within the denominations for the first time since the sixteenth century. . . . "This finally brings a close to that separation," said John Thomas. . . . "This is an encouragement to look beyond congregational isolation" (*Walla Walla Union Bulletin*, July 6, 1997).

Peter Wagner, the church growth guru, has recently conducted a postdenominationalism convention where ministers of many denominations united in a precursor to an ecumenism that prior movements have never accomplished. Today many of our young generation Xer's are parroting this lack of commitment to our church. We are experiencing an identity crisis. Two of our top conference youth directors were recently in my office and told me that they see some of the sharpest academy and college kids as good Christians, but showing little commitment to the specific calling of our Adventist message. Maybe that shouldn't come as a surprise.

According to the ten-year longitudinal study by Bailey Gillespie and Stu Tyner, 80 percent of twenty-five- to twenty-seven-year olds have a relatively high acceptance of many key Adventist doctrines and are "very certain" or "quite certain" they want to stay in the church. But:

- Only 56 percent attend church regularly.
- Only 44 percent pay tithe.
- Seventy-eight percent hold no office in the church.
- Less than 30 percent have family worship at least once per week.

Many have an identity in the Adventist Church. They have been socialized into the church, but they don't translate this theological belief system into institutional commitment.

If we were once guilty, as a church, of emphasizing Adventism at the expense of a grace orientation and a love for Christ, we must not now fall into the other ditch of raising a generation of Adventists with no commitment to the God-given role of Advent- ism. A correct grace orientation is not in conflict with the fundamentals of Adventism. The two are not mutually exclusive as some would have us believe.

But, leaders, even with its theology intact, this church would not be a great church without its organizational structure. One cannot work or even travel around the world church without seeing the necessity of our organization and financial system.

God raised up the Seventh-day Adventist Church to accomplish something that no other denomination is prepared to do. You see, when God gave our church its theology; He also gave it a practical organizational structure. As a part of my doctoral dissertation I did some study into the development of that structure. How our early church leaders hammered it out makes for some pretty fascinating reading. But the development of the organizational structure was inspired by the same Designer that inspired our doctrines.

Now, I am painfully aware that we can become bureaucratic and overinstitutionalized. There is a possibility that our corporate church can become overly corporate in appearance and function. With world-class educational institutions, publishing houses, medical institutions, and conference/union offices, there is the danger that we begin getting our self-image from our institutions rather than from our mission. There is the danger that we allow these outstanding and irreplaceable institutions to become an end in themselves rather than a means to an end.

Joshua V. Himes, William Miller's second in command, wrote to Ellen White in 1895:

> You have many good and great things connected with
> health reform and the churches, with the increase of wealth,
> and colleges as well, and to me it looks like work in all these
> departments that may go on for a long time to come. . . .

There is a great and earnest work being done to send the message of the third angel everywhere—but all classes of Adventists are prospering in worldly things, and heaping up riches, while they talk of the coming of Christ as an event very near at hand. It is a great thing to be consistent and true to the real Advent message (quoted by George Knight, "Adventism at 150," *Ministry,* October 1994, p. 13).

So there are cautions we need to hear, but the words of Ellen White in 1893 are still valid:

Let none entertain the thought, however, that we can dispense with organization. It has cost us much study, and many prayers for wisdom that we know God has answered, to erect this structure. It has been built up by His direction, through much sacrifice and conflict. Let none of our brethren be so deceived as to attempt to tear it down; for you will thus bring in a condition of things that you do not dream of. In the name of the Lord, I declare to you that it is to stand, strengthened, established, and settled. At God's command, "Go forward," we advanced when the difficulties to be surmounted made the advance seem impossible. We know how much it has cost to work out God's plan in the past, which has made us as a people what we are. Then let every one be exceedingly careful not to unsettle minds in regard to these things that God has ordained for our prosperity and success in advancing His cause (*General Conference Bulletin,* April 10, 1903).

Does our church organization have flaws today? Certainly. Since people like you and me are leading this church, it would naturally have weaknesses. But I feel sorry for those who spend their energies focusing on the *sins* of God's people rather than focusing on the *Savior* of God's people. But be that as it may, after acknowledging the defects of our church and its organizational structure, just try to name a denominational structure of which you would rather be a part. I praise God for our "faulty and defective" church. And I believe it is still "the one object upon which God bestows in a special sense His supreme regard" (*The Acts of the Apostles,* p. 12).

OUR MISSION

When God had given our church a clear system of theology and guidance in the erecting of its organizational structure, we were poised for our prophetic mission. Yes, it is a mission that is different from that of any other denomination. In some small churches that are split by dissension and locked into the status quo, you may find it hard to focus on mission. It is hard to get excited about draining the swamp when you're up to your ears in alligators. But the Seventh-day Adventist Church is alive, vibrant, and exploding in growth. I know that the cynics will say we're not growing as fast as is the population. But look at it another way. In 1870, there was one Adventist for every 250,552 people in the world. At the current rate of growth, projections suggest that by the end of the year 2030 there will be one Adventist for every 134 persons in the world. And according to Adherents.com, one of the most prestigious Internet resources for church statistics, Seventh-day Adventists are now the eighth largest international religious body.

Our church organizes four and a half new churches per day around the world! One baptism occurs every 28.93 seconds! Adventism now has a presence in all the parts of the world with the exception of a handful of countries; Adventist World Radio is beaming the message on all continents; evangelism satellite down-link capability reaches all over the world. Yes, God is using His church mightily!

The mission of our church will not be accomplished by copying some of the fast-growing congregational churches of today. Of course, we should borrow the legitimate aspects and take the principles that are supported by the Bible and Spirit of Prophecy. But remember there is a basic philosophical difference between our church and the model on which many of the superchurches are patterned. We believe and practice systematic benevolence—a system of financial sharing in order to accomplish an otherwise impossible worldwide task. And we believe that a wonderful reflex action takes place as a result, that helps our local work as well. The way to strengthen the local church program is to promote overseas missions.

Our worldwide mission emphasis is phenomenal. Our educational system is the largest Protestant system in the world. Most of the large superchurches in American society today don't run colleges, academies, elementary schools, youth camps, or promote a worldwide mission program because they feel it is not cost effective. Seventh-day Adventists do these things. And all of that is to say nothing of the major differences between us and other churches in the areas of doctrine and prophecy.

I'll never forget that in one conference of which I was president, we realized an increase to our regular offerings and tithe went up 26 percent—all during the peak of a major overseas mission project in which the conference was involved. Our members were revitalized spiritually. During that same period of time, critical independent ministries lost momentum. That's God's way. That's the Spirit of Prophecy way. That's the Adventist way.

So here we are as God's last-day remnant church, standing in the gap, making a difference. It's tough. These are difficult times. Cynics are noting the delay of Christ's coming and are challenging our historic understanding of last-day events.

Recently in family worship, while reading the *Story of Redemption,* we read how Moses was told that he would deliver the children of Israel from Egypt. The elders also were told that Moses was chosen to deliver the children of Israel. After nearly four hundred years of captivity there was great expectation. Then it appeared that God's plan was foiled. Imagine the disappointment. Imagine the cynicism, particularly toward the leaders who had predicted the coming of a deliverer. But the lesson to be learned is this: When it gets the bleakest, when things are seemingly impossible, God is at His best, working behind the scenes. And you can be assured, even when He has to go to plan "B," that Plan B is not ineffective. Oh, we may lose some battles, but remember God *always* wins the war. And despite the critics, the cynics, the obstructionists, and the revisionists—even in spite of all of Pharaoh's army—Moses most certainly did lead the children of Israel out of Egypt just as predicted.

Here's an incredible quotation I just came across a few days ago:

> The Lord has allowed matters in our day to come to a crisis, in the exaltation of error above truth, that He, the God of Israel, might work mightily for the greater elevation of His truth in proportion as error is exalted.

> With His eye upon the church, the Lord has again and again allowed matters to come to a crisis, that in their extremity His people should look alone for His help. . . . God reserves His gracious interposition in their behalf till the time of their extremity; thus He makes their deliverance more

marked, and their victories more glorious (*Selected Messages*, bk. 2, p. 372.)

PRAISE THE LORD!

In the Ellen White biographies I've come across one of the experiences of A. G. Daniels that is of particular interest to leaders. Prior to the General Conference session Daniels was weary from the conflict of trying to hold things together in general and particularly as the conflict related to attacks upon Ellen White. Just before the General Conference session began, he set aside the Sabbath for personal fasting and prayer.

In recounting the story just a few hours before his death, he said, "I struggled unto death, crying aloud, and I nearly reproached the Lord for not giving me some sign, some evidence of my acceptance, and His support of me in the awful battle that was before us." During this struggle he prostrated himself on the floor, clutching, as it were, at the floorboards as he agonized with God. All night he wrestled with the Lord. Then, he reports, as the morning sun burst into the room, "As distinctly as if audibly spoken, the words burned into my mind as a message from heaven, 'If you will stand by My servant until her sun sets in a bright sky, I will stand by you to the last hour of the conflict' " (Arthur White, *Ellen G. White: The Early Elmshaven Years 1900-1905*, vol. 5, p. 240).

Later that year, the debate over pantheism became more agitated in the church. In dealing with the issue, Dr. Paulson shook his finger at Elder Daniels and said,

"You are making the mistake of your life. After all this turmoil, some of these days you will wake up and find your-self rolled in the dust, and another will be leading the forces." Elder Daniels straightened up in his weariness and discour-agement and replied firmly, "I do not believe your prophecy. At any rate I would rather be rolled in the dust doing what I believe in my soul to be right than to walk with princes doing what my conscience tells me is wrong" (Ibid., p. 297).

What a powerful testimony! What a model for us as leaders!

I praise God for His plan. He raised up our prophetic church by inspiring its *theology,* which drives its *mission,* made possible by its *organization.* And incredibly He has entrusted all this into feeble hands like yours and mine. I am humbled and eternally grateful for this realization. I pray that we will be willing to accept this chal-lenge. I close this chapter with a familiar thought from Ellen White:

> In reviewing our past history, having traveled over every step of advance to our present standing, I can say, Praise God! As I see what the Lord has wrought, I am filled with astonish-ment, and with confidence in Christ as leader. We have nothing to fear for the future, except as we shall forget the way the Lord has led us, and His teaching in our past history (*Life Sketches,* p. 196).

"It is much more important to do the right thing
than to do things right."
—*Peter Drucker.*

"If you would lift me, you must be on higher ground!
If you would lead me, you must be ahead of me."
—*Anonymous.*

CHAPTER 2

QUALITIES OF A CHRISTIAN LEADER

He was seventeen years old, good looking, wealthy, talented, and overly self-confident. Joseph, son of Jacob, reminded himself many times of his good qualities as he tramped through the miles of expansive grasslands.

He had been sent to check on his ten recalcitrant brothers. Once before he had returned to his father with a disparaging report about them. But perhaps by now they had changed. Joseph, however, was so caught up in his own good fortune he was oblivious to their feelings.

Knowing the animosity Shechemites had toward nomads like his family, Joseph had avoided their community. Not being able to locate his brothers, he wandered through the pasture land and noted another striking evidence of providential leading in his life. With incredible "coincidence" he met a man who had overheard his brothers say they were going to Dothan. It had already been a fifty-mile walk to Shechem; now it would be another fifteen miles to Dothan. *Those brothers had better appreciate my visit,* Joseph thought, as he trudged on wrapped in his multicolored robe.

Like Muhammed Ali, the world heavyweight champion who could hardly wait to get up in the morning so he could see himself in the mirror, Joseph was proud. If you read the biblical account carefully, he came by it rather naturally. Jacob vicariously lived out his own ambitions through this son of his favorite wife.

And you male readers know that if we're honest, we'll have to admit we all do that a bit—like the T-shirt that says, "The older I get, the better I was." As Jacob sat around bragging to his old cronies about this son of his old age, you can hear him say, "So you guys didn't think I had it in me, huh? Well let me tell you—there may be snow on the roof, but there's fire in the hearth!"

PRIDE

So, as leaders, the first lesson that we must learn before we can be effectively used by God is the lesson that Joseph had to learn— pride goes before a fall. Pride is the root of almost all our problems. Pride caused the downfall of Lucifer, and pride is the one socially "acceptable" sin even among church leaders.

What is pride? Essentially it is an unwillingness to submit. The whole Christian life is based on submission—wives to husbands, husbands to wives, one church member to another, and all of us to Christ and the authority He vests in His church, including keeping the seventh day holy, not the sixth, returning the tithe into the storehouse, not just to some worthy project of our choice.

Paul dealt with this same issue in the early church when he addressed the matter of meat offered to idols. He said that some things may be legal, but not expedient. And of course Christ's life was the quintessential role model of the humble, submissive leader.

But that was a lesson Joseph had yet to learn. He would eventually brutally encounter the consequences of pride, but for now he was oblivious to that fact due to his singular concentration on his bright destiny. If anyone challenged the fact of his "specialness," he would remind them of his dreams. Just thinking about them made him walk a little straighter, imagining those sheaves and the sun, moon, and stars bowing down to him.

Upon locating his brothers, Joseph quickly realized he had created a major problem. In no way does that excuse the brothers' response, of course. Selling their brother into a life of slavery was a dastardly deed. But in a very real sense Joseph had brought it on himself through his own pride. And Joseph would reap the devastating consequences.

As he assessed the situation and determined his destiny, he realized that slavery was a worse fate than death. He pleaded with his brothers to release him, if not for his sake at least for their father's, but to no avail. So the caravan, including the camel carrying its unwilling baggage, headed toward Egypt. As the distant hills that housed his father's tent faded into the sunset, so did any residual pride in the young Joseph.

As leaders we must learn that lesson personally—and we must learn it corporately. Christ said of our church today:

> These are the words of the Amen, the faithful and true witness, the ruler of God's creation…. You say, "I am rich; I have acquired wealth and do not need a thing." But you do not realize that you are wretched, pitiful, poor, blind and naked. I counsel you to buy from me gold refined in the fire, so you can become rich; and white clothes to wear, so you can cover your shameful nakedness; and salve to put on your eyes, so you can see (Revelation 3:14, 17, 18, NIV).

One of my favorite quotations is found in *Early Writings,* page 119. "If pride and selfishness were laid aside, five minutes would remove most difficulties." Remember that the next time you are chairing a committee that is split over some insignificant issue.

As Joseph rode mile after mile, he began to think. For the first time he clearly saw the reality of the age-old truth, pride does indeed go before a fall. Now as the pyramids of Egypt loomed ahead, Joseph saw clearly the folly of his pride. He began this trip as a proud seventeen-year-old boy and ended it as a humble seventeen-year-old man. He had learned the first of three important lessons—the lesson of the consequence of pride.

PRINCIPLE

Joseph was taken to the market place and sold on the auction block like a common animal. There Potiphar, Pharaoh's official captain of the guard, bought him. Joseph had options as to how he would respond at that point. He chose to remain true to principle. This is lesson number two for the leader in training. A lesser man would have said, "I've been deserted by my family, forsaken by my God; when in Egypt, do as the Egyptians do."

The pen of inspiration wrote of Joseph:

He was in the midst of idolatry. The worship of false gods was surrounded by all the pomp of royalty, supported by the wealth and culture of the most highly civilized nation then in existence. Yet Joseph preserved his simplicity and his fidelity to God (Ellen G. White, *Patriarchs and Prophets,* p. 214).

For its time, Egypt was a modern society with an amoral culture. Don't believe for a moment that there wasn't enticement for this lonely teenager. Ellen White continues:

> The sights and sounds of vice were all about him, but he was as one who saw and heard not. His thoughts were not permitted to linger upon forbidden subjects. The desire to gain the favor of the Egyptians could not cause him to conceal his principles. Had he attempted to do this, he would have been overcome by temptation; but he was not ashamed of the religion of his fathers, and he made no effort to hide the fact that he was a worshiper of Jehovah (Ibid.).

But even this determination was no guarantee against temptation. His unusual beauty and diligence did not go unnoticed by Potiphar's wife. The Bible is pretty descriptive:

> So [Potiphar] left in Joseph's care everything he had; with Joseph in charge, he did not concern himself with anything except the food he ate. Now Joseph was well-built and handsome, and after a while his master's wife took notice of Joseph and said, "Come to bed with me!" But he refused. "With me in charge," he told her, "my master does not concern himself with anything in the house; everything he owns he has entrusted to my care. No one is greater in this house than I am. My master has withheld nothing from me except you, because you are his wife. How then could I do such a wicked thing and sin against God?" And though she spoke to Joseph day after day, he refused to go to bed with her or even be with her (Genesis 39:6-10, NIV).

Egyptologists and archeologists verify that the ancient Egyptian women were some of the first to consider themselves liberated women. Egyptian monuments testify to the laxity of morals. Thus Potiphar's wife's shameless proposition.

Notice that the Bible records that "day after day" she tempted him. It is significant to note that the same expression is also used to describe a similar situation with drastically different results. Judges 16:16 says that Delilah came to Sampson "day after day" (NIV) trying to wheedle from him the secret of his great strength. Samson eventually gave in. But in Joseph's case, the Bible records that he refused to go to bed with Potiphar's wife or even to be with her.

Then came the moment of truth. The historian Josephus tells us that it was festival time. Potiphar was called away to the king's palace while Mrs. Potiphar pretended to be sick, thereby being able to stay at home with Joseph.

This time her advances were premeditated, calculating, and determined. She promised him concealment, favors, and rewards.

If he refused he would face disgrace, imprisonment, and possibly death.

The success or failure of Joseph to stand for principle during the moment of supreme temptation was dependent upon his earlier preparation. It was his daily connection with God that would predict the outcome of this intense seduction.

Too often when there is a moral fall by a leader, the excuse is made that it was just a careless moment of indiscretion. Don't kid yourself. Too often the mind has been conditioned for failure. Leaders have allowed themselves to become de-sensitized by their own choices. In the area of moral integrity, if the truth were known, the preamble for an illicit affair often begins with the curse of the twenty-first century—pornography. And unfortunately church leaders are special targets.

Did you know that:

• The number of people who visit Internet sex sites in the United States *each day* is estimated at sixty million?

• Together, the top five U. S. sex sites have more Internet visits than MSNBC.com or CNN.com combined?

• Every day approximately 400 new porn Web sites open on the Internet from locations as far a way as Thailand and Russia?

It's like the old saying, "Garbage in, garbage out."

George Eliot wrote, "The Devil tempts us not. It is we who tempt him, beckoning his skill with opportunity." In other words when the inevitable moments of decision come, the eternal consequences of a momentous decision are predicated on what has been programmed into the mind.

We can see young Joseph running from Potiphar's wife shouting over his shoulder, "I'd rather be in prison with God than in bed with you!"

There is a fascinating story that comes out of the assassination of President John Kennedy that speaks to these critical decisions of a moment. Clint Hill was the Secret Service agent responsible for the president's protection that day in Dallas, Texas. He was riding on the hood of the car immediately behind the presidential limousine. When the first shot was fired he jumped from the slowly moving vehicle, raced to the president, and covered his body with his own.

Years later on national television Hill admitted to the American public that there could have been a significantly different outcome had he acted differently in the moment of crisis. Timed film clips of the event show that Hill was on top of the presidential limousine just 2.5 seconds after the assassin's first shot. But Hill confessed that had he responded one-half of a second sooner history might have been rewritten. Years later—and many psychiatric counseling visits later—he was still coping with the guilt of a moment's decision.

It is interesting that Ellen White uses the same wording as she describes Joseph's crisis. "His whole future life depended upon the decision of the moment. Would principle triumph? Would Joseph still be true to God? With inexpressible anxiety, angels looked upon the scene" (*Patriarchs and Prophets,* p. 217).

And so Joseph, having shut out the sights and sounds of vice about him, successfully passed the test of standing for principle. This didn't mean, however, that he would have no more trials. Joseph had one more lesson he needed to learn to become a great leader.

PERSEVERANCE

As he spent the next few years in prison for his moral decisions Joseph could have easily succumbed to self-pity and blaming God. A lesser man would have said, "OK, God, when I was sold into slavery that was my fault. I was rather proud. But this time I did what was right. I stood for principle. And where did it get me?"

But Joseph trusted God. He demonstrated his integrity and work ethic and eventually was placed second in command, next to Pharaoh. He was ultimately able to be a tremendous witness for his God. Additionally, he became the savior of the country as well as his own family during the famine.

He had become a leader who epitomized the best in personal perseverance. We don't know how many years Joseph spent in prison, but we do know that it was two long years after the butler promised he would remember Joseph to Pharaoh before he was released. Oswald Chambers defines perseverance wonderfully in his classic work, *My Utmost for His Highest.* He says:

> Perseverance is more than endurance. It is combined with absolute assurance that what we are hoping for is going to happen. Endurance may merely be the fear of letting go. Perseverance demonstrates complete faith that God will prevail. If our hopes are experiencing disappointment, it is because they are being purified (p. 22).

There is an interesting postscript to this great story, which demonstrates how God blesses those who are faithful to Him. The Bible records that Joseph married a beautiful young Egyptian woman by the name of Asenath by which he had two sons—Manasseth whose name means, "God has made me forget all my troubles," and Ephraim, "God has made me fruitful in the land of my suffering."

But the point usually overlooked is that Asenath was the daughter of Potiphera who according to the historian, Josephus, translators of the Septuagent, and numerous Hebrew scholars, was none other than the same Potiphar, Joseph's slave master! This was an eventuality that only God could have orchestrated!

Joseph must have gotten acquainted with her, possibly fallen in love with her, when he worked for her father many years before. As a slave, he could only dream that someday he could marry this official's daughter—and his childhood sweetheart.

So through this familiar story of Joseph, one of the great leaders in history, we learn the three lessons that are required of God's leaders still today.

"The best way to predict the future is to invent it."
—*Alca Kay,* scientist, inventor.

"We will find a way or make one."
—*Hannibal,* when he was trying to get his elephants over the Alps.

CHAPTER 3

VISION

A few years ago, I had to speak at a convention that had for its theme: *Magnify the vision.* That got me to thinking. There is an inherent challenge to that slogan. The Bible itself says: "Where there is no vision, the people perish" (Proverbs 29:18, KJV). And while seeing is believing and believing is achieving, we might also say that believing is the first step to seeing.

If our church were ever to die, it wouldn't be because of attacks from the self-righteousness of the radical right or from the Laodicea of the liberal left. It would be because those of us leaders in the middle of the road have lost our vision.

One frustrated Methodist leader stated, "The Methodist Church has all the vision of a wiperless windshield in the middle of a squall!" May that never be said of our church. But to make certain that never happens we must constantly recognize that times are changing.

Bill Gates in his bestseller, *Business @ The Speed of Thought,* says, "If the 1980's were about quality, and the 1990's were about re-engineering, then the 2000's will be about velocity. About how quickly the nature of business will change" (p. xiii).

Then we church leaders had better not plan to do business as usual.

REMEMBER OUR ROOTS

If we are going to magnify the vision for the future, then we had better not forget where we came from.

A few paragraphs above, I used the analogy of an automobile in a squall. Let's use the automobile again to illustrate a point. When I am driving down the road, I had better occasionally check the rear view mirror to see where I've been. On the rear view mirror of my car are the words, "Objects may be closer than they appear." Likewise the lessons of our past—our failings and our triumphs— should not be relegated to the distant past. "Discover it again for the first time" and "going back to the future" should be more than clever advertising jingles.

We can have confidence for the future *only* as we do not forget how He has led us in our past recent history. And that would include:

- The fundamentals of our doctrines.
- The pillars of our faith.
- The providential history of our beginnings.

And the beautiful insights of the Spirit of Prophecy given by that great visionary Ellen White must ever guide our vision for the future.

KEEP THE FOCUS

Anytime you try to magnify a vision you run the risk of losing the focus. As leaders in the church, you and I must constantly be adjusting the focus. It is increasingly easy for a multiethnic, multi-lingual, multicultural, multigenerational church to have so many programs that the fundamental focus of God's remnant church can be lost. There are good things that can sap our energy and re-sources yet not contribute to the direct accomplishment of the mission of this church. Sharing the good news of Jesus Christ is still the only rationale for the existence of the prophetic remnant church.

According to the Billy Graham organization only 4 percent of American churches are evangelistic in their orientation. While Adventist churches may have a higher percent that are involved in directly spreading the gospel to an unreached world, I've seen too many that do little or nothing to fulfill the Great Commission.

Let's not forget we have indeed been fed to feed, led to lead, and blessed to be a blessing.

UNITED WE STAND

Finally, if we are to magnify the vision in the twenty-first cen-tury, we must do it with a renewed sense of unity. At the same convention I mentioned at the beginning of this chapter, I learned that the organizers had ordered a shipment of ballpoint pens for the delegates. The pens were to be imprinted with the convention's theme—"Magnify the Vision." The first batch arrived with the erroneously imprinted words, "Magnify Division." Needless to say they sent the pens back. There's no room for "division" in this church. And we certainly don't want to magnify any we do have. We cannot continue to carelessly disenfranchise any segment of this church.

We need the energy of the young people. We need the strength of our women. We need the creativity of our progressives. We need the fervor of our conservatives. And we need the insights of our former members.

Former president Bill Clinton once made a rather insightful statement. "I learned," he said, "you'll be useless in politics if you have no vision. But you can also be rendered useless if you ignore everybody else's vision." In other words, we need each other.

And whether it is theology or polity, this church has a tradition of strength because it has a tradition of unity, despite its lack of uniformity. When the family speaks, the members of that family had better listen. Today thousands are being dashed against the rocks of isolationism, dying from a lack of fellowship, and drawn into the whirlpool of individualism. And the coral reef of sin is littered with the shipwrecks of those who have ignored the wise man's advice, "In the multitude of counselors there is safety" (Proverbs 11:14, NKJV). It is worth noting that when God decided to provide a way of salvation for Noah and his family, He said, "Build an ark." He didn't say, "Build a thousand canoes." That was so they would be safe together.

So today we do well to focus on the past yet at the same time magnify the vision for the future.

As Christian leaders we may have received a call from a particular individual or organization to work for that person or that organization. But more significantly, we have to believe that it was a call from *God*. And we need to respond appropriately.

Oswald Chambers said, "It is easier to work for God without a vision and without a call because then you are not bothered by what He requires."

But we know that God does have requirements for His leaders. Therefore I challenge you to intentionally accept God's call to be a visionary leader.

"If the highest aim of a captain were to preserve his ship,
he would keep it in port forever."
—*St. Thomas Aquinas.*

"Those who occupy positions of influence and responsibility
in the church, should be foremost in the work of God. . . .
When their light burns brightly, a thousand torches
will be kindled at the flame."
—*Ellen G. White, Signs of the Times,* December 6, 1883.

CHAPTER 4

I D.A.R.E. YOU

Leaders and the organizations they represent are under constant attack, criticism, and ridicule. It's reached the point that almost all leaders are perceived as bumbling bozos of the bureaucracy. Possibly even worse is the perception that leaders are overpaid and underworked—each scratching the other's back, with pork barrel politics being practiced within the church as well as without, each leader cunningly conniving to perpetuate his or her power base while marking time until the next paycheck arrives.

I was disgusted by an ad I received recently promoting a sinister book for executives. It was titled, *The Black Book of Executive Politics, an Infighter's Guide to Survival—and Success.* Contents:

- "How to Make People Tell the Truth"
- "Ways to Throw Low Blows That Can Never be Tracked Back to You"
- "Setting Up a Rival to Fall on His Face"
- "How to Derail a Lecher's Career With a Sexual Harassment Charge"

- "How to Get Credit for Other People's Work"
- "Subtle Ways to Kick Your Enemies When They're Down—So They Don't Get Up Again"
- "How to Use Sexual Suggestions to Get Your Way"

It's no wonder that leaders' credibility is being called into question.

Due to the credibility gap in leadership, the competition of the Japanese, and/or just plain survival in a worsening economy, there is a heightened awareness in the business world today that business cannot go on as usual. Furthermore, change is taking place at a laser-fast pace, and only those who are a part of it will survive. Only those who themselves are change agents will be successful leaders.

A great example of sticking to the conventional game plan in times of change occurred in football at the turn of the century. In 1905 football was a low-scoring game of running and kicking. Then in 1906, the forward pass was legalized, making it possible to gain forty yards in an instant. Still, during the first season most teams stayed with the conventional wisdom—what was tried and true.

However, the St. Louis University coach Eddie Cochems realized they were in a new era and that "three yards and a cloud of dust" was now obsolete. The team got a vision of what could happen with the new passing game that season and outscored their opponents 402-11! That's what I'm suggesting for the game of life.

Lee Iacocca says, "I have to take risks every day; I'd rather not, but the world doesn't give me this option." Bank of America senior vice president, Shelly Porges says: "To keep ahead in this dynamic environment . . . requires more than a change in structure, it requires a whole new way of thinking."

I want to suggest that many of these back-to-basics principles are likewise valuable for the church. They are valuable for some of the same reasons that apply in the business world, but they are also valuable to the church for an even more important reason— because we are in the people-saving business. And if, as the Bible predicts, the devil is going about as a roaring lion, and if, as Ellen G. White states, he is ten times more effective today than in the times of the apostles, then our competition demands that we church leaders must be every bit as wise as our worldly counterparts. The Bible puts it this way: "For the children of this world are more astute in dealing with their own kind than are the children of light" (Luke 16:8, *The Jerusalem Bible*).

Let me suggest four principles that are basic, yet contemporary state-of-the-art thinking in today's business environment—applicable to the largest corporation or the smallest church. I keep them in mind with the acronym D.A.R.E.

DREAM

It has been said many times, "He who aims at nothing is sure to hit it." Or as the old Indian saying puts it, "It is better to aim your spear at the moon and hit an eagle than to aim at an eagle and hit a rock."

The Bible says it this way: "Where there is no vision, the people perish" (Proverbs 29:18, KJV). And while seeing may be believing, believing is the first step to seeing.

President Bill Clinton said in a *Newsweek* interview, "I learned the hard way when I was defeated in the 1980 governor's race that you have to really have priorities and make them clear to people. If you do a zillion things, even if you do them well, people may perceive that you haven't done anything."

It isn't the inept that destroy an organization; the incompetent don't often get into a position where they can make a significant impact. Those who destroy an organization are those who once achieved success, but who want to rest on their achievements, thereby causing a drift toward mediocrity.

As leaders, we need *vision,* and we need *passion!* Michael Liacko, vice president of sales for Bell & Howell, was asked which individuals make the best salespeople. He went to the flip chart and drew a vertical line on the left, listing the requisite basic skills: product knowledge, competitors' strategy, good background in electronics, degree in marketing—all the usual criteria.

Then on the right side of the chart he wrote: "Fire in the Heart." Then he said, "If I have to choose between someone with the résumé and the educational background versus someone with fire, I'd pick the one with fire." People with fire are more motivated, resilient, resourceful, and will work harder.

The bottom line is that good is not good enough. Degrees aren't sufficient. Leaders need passion, fire in the heart, burning commitment, and desire. These are the qualities that move a leader from good to outstanding, from mediocrity to success, from status quo to exceptional performance.

Today I'd definitely characterize our world church as a good, solid organization. Our conferences are good conferences. Our churches are good churches. Stability is one of the greatest strengths, but can also be a liability. We have many key indicators to prove that our church is a good, solid organization. But we're not as great as we could be. And as leaders we can look only to ourselves. We can't blame anyone else—not even the critics, the skeptics, and the muckrakers. We have to begin to dream dreams and see visions. I D.A.R.E. you to start dreaming today!

ARTICULATE

The second of these four basic fundamentals is "articulate." Today in the church we are spending an inordinate time dealing with the conservatives and liberals. It's been said that a conservative is one who acts without thinking, and a liberal is one who thinks without acting. A conservative sacrifices relevance for revelation, and a liberal sacrifices revelation for relevance.

I want to suggest that if we are ever going to mobilize these two distinct elements into a complementary, unified force it is by articulating a higher goal. When one organization that I was a part of began a concerted effort to do global mission, we saw a dramatic reduction in the number of critical independent ministries and break-away congregational churches.

The role of a leader is to articulate a vision with enthusiasm. Or as someone has said, "A leader is a person who takes people to a place they wouldn't go by themselves." The spiritual implications are obvious.

You're a leader! How many people have you led in the last year to make a decision that will take them to a place they wouldn't go by themselves?

As a leader, you are a thermostat, not a thermometer; you are a hammer, not an anvil.

Let's stop being consensus builders and managers and become leaders. Join the ranks of the Martin Luthers, the John Knoxs, the Mother Teresas.

Be a paradigm shifter, a change agent. And let's begin fulfilling prophecy by our old men and women dreaming dreams, and our young men and women seeing visions.

REALIZE

The third basic principle I'd like to D.A.R.E. you to practice is to "realize."

On Tuesday, October 17, 1989, at 5:04 P.M. Pacific Daylight Time, the earth began to shake under the San Francisco Bay area. In what was then named Candlestick Park, the Oakland Athletics and the San Francisco Giants baseball teams were getting ready to begin the World Series.

Suddenly in that great stadium the lights began to flicker. Steel girders holding the upper deck began to sway, and pieces of concrete started crumbling down. A voice over the loud speaker told spectators to leave. But when the initial quake was over, fans began shouting, "Play ball!"

In the Marina district north of Candlestick Park, houses shifted off crumbling foundations, and buildings collapsed. Gas lines exploded, and fires broke out. Across the Bay, in Oakland, a mile-long section of Highway 880 fell, crushing rush-hour commuters. In the course of one minute thousands of peoples' lives were changed because of something that happened deep inside the earth, and merely shouting "Play ball!" would not change these cataclysmic forces.

No, there must be a strategy. This will involve pain, trial, error, and failure, but the impact can be enormous.

Deciding to change—having a vision—is only half of the battle. We have to develop a workable strategy to take people with us. And that is difficult as we all know.

Some of us have spent so much energy developing and pursuing goals and objectives that once we've achieved what we planned to do, we're too tired to ever really see or envision the bigger picture. Too many people are interested in doing things right instead of doing right things. Too many strategies become an end in themselves.

Summing up the fixation on short-term objectives, Scott McNeally, CEO of Sun Microsystems, said that the motto at his company (the second fastest growing company in economic history) is, "Goals only limit you!"

Does that mean that we shouldn't have goals or objectives? Absolutely not! I believe in goals. But they should never become an end in themselves or the results will be short lived.

The key to sustained high performance is not focusing on a goal, but on something larger than a goal—something bigger to stand for. Something that inspires and motivates a dream you can dream.

When Jesus was here on earth, He didn't say, "Let's set a goal of 3,000 to be baptized on one day," and then spend three years planning a strategy to achieve that goal. Rather, He said, "Let's tell the world the good news, and then I will come back."

Our early church leaders never spent time dreaming about baptizing twenty million into the fledgling Adventist Church. They dreamed about the Second Coming and how near it was.

And they went out and worked . . . hard . . . effectively. The disciples combined the functions of the right hemisphere of the brain and the left. The right hemisphere houses dreams, passion, and imagination. Goals, on the other hand, are found in the left hemisphere. It's the balance of the two that have made people successful long before they knew or cared about right and left hemispheres.

Today your organization, your church, will need to begin to change. If we are to reach the unreached, church the unchurched, and save the unsaved, we must realize that the average nonattending baby boomer or baby buster doesn't want to live in the twenty-first century six days a week, and then come to a Sabbath School, church service, or evangelistic meeting that has all the trappings of the 1970s.

You've heard about the lay leader who introduced the new pastor to the church by saying, "He is someone who can lead this church into the twentieth century." Someone seated on the platform whispered, "You mean the twenty-first century." To which the lay leader replied, "No. As out of touch as this church is I'd be glad to get it into the twentieth century!"

As leaders, we must be enablers. We must provide a pathway to the promise.

Engen Lang graduated in 1933 from Harlem P.S. 121. In 1981, as a successful, wealthy business man, he was invited back to speak to the sixth graders for their commencement address. He changed his speech on the spot.

"I had a dream," he told them. "Martin Luther King had a dream. Everyone must have a dream. But a dream isn't enough. You must be willing to work and sacrifice and study and go on to college if you want to be successful.

"To let you know I'm serious about what I say," he continued, "I will provide a scholarship to every one of you who graduates from high school."

The students left that auditorium with the cheers of the audience and the challenge of a leader ringing in their ears.

In the past, 25 percent of the students at Harlem P.S. 121 graduated from high school. But of that class, which had been given a vision—coupled with a pathway to the promise—forty-eight out of fifty-two students graduated from high school!

As church leaders, you and I must be more than cheerleaders; we must be enablers. We must be change agents.

Now this can be risky business. It doesn't take a whole lot of spirituality to change a church. Change merely for change's sake is seldom, if ever, valid. Leadership by destabilization may work for a while, but as the Germans found out in the 1940s and the Russians learned in the 1930s, it does not have lasting, positive results. The apostle Paul was willing to become all things to all people, but he was also unwilling to compromise his mission even if he were beaten, starved, or shipwrecked.

There must always be a list of non-negotiables because the sacrifice of compromise is too great. Therefore, as leaders, we must have one ear tuned to God and one ear to the people's needs.

In recent years there has been much talk about paradigm shifts. It is a good concept. A paradigm is a set of rules and regulations—either implied or explicit—that (1) defines boundaries, and (2) tells you what to do to be successful within those boundaries. On a practical note rather than a moral one, are the poor leaders who begin advocating change before they have earned the right to change. Change happens slowly, carefully, and lovingly. There are many good ideas that never have gotten off the ground because that principle was ignored.

Every viable company has a mission statement. And every viable organization, likewise, has reached that mission statement through a process that has enlisted the ownership of the members of that organization. I hope you regularly monitor mission statements and amend goals and objectives. This can do much to unify your organization and marshal its energies. Management guru, Peter Drucker, says, "When there is understanding, there is unity even if there isn't agreement." Taking your organization through a process of defining and setting objectives will mobilize its members and bring unity. And then they are ready to go forward, to advance, to accomplish. Yes, to realize.

As someone quipped about his own church that needed to get past the planning stage to the realization state: "We need to have a five-day plan to stop planning." Nike's motto—"Just do it!"—is good for church leaders too. It was Tom Peters, known for the pursuit of excellence, who said, "Ready, fire, aim." Many of our church entities are big on sitting around and naval gazing.

Everything we do should be in the context of our vision that Jesus is coming soon. Check the visions because they focus on one of two ways—either inward or outward. That's radical but that's biblical. And if we don't begin doing this, we will die as a church.

Management experts Peter Lorange and Robert Nelson list early warning signs for corporations headed for trouble. These are applicable to our church organizations as well:

• Excess personnel.
• Cumbersome procedures.
• Replacement of substance with form.
• And tolerance of incompetence.

This last one we'll discuss briefly later.

Specifically addressing the church, George Barna of Barna Research Group says, "The church in America has shown little forward progress over the past decade." Based on a five-year study of 100,000 American churches, Barna identified as the "top ill-nesses" in the church:

- Pastors are ill equipped by seminaries to run the church business.
- Christians fail to hold each other accountable to Christian living.
- Christians haven't targeted special audiences with personalized messages.
- Churches spend five times as much money on buildings and maintenance as they do on promoting evangelism.

Does that analysis fit your church? Your organization?

Let's go back to where we started. A poll of America's Fortune 500 CEOs asked them to identify the characteristics of top leaders in the decade to come. The number one response? Vision. If that's true, then we leaders need to get going and growing. Someone said there are two ways to get to the top of an oak tree. Grab a limb and start climbing—or sit on an acorn and wait till it grows. You see, even if you're on the right track, you'll get run over if you don't get moving.

Will we experience failures? Certainly. Set backs? For sure. But, as leaders, our job is *not* to find people doing something wrong, but to make heroes out of them. I once offered fifty dollars to any pastor in our conference who during the following year would try something creative—that failed!

At first, you may feel like Elijah—the only voice. So be it. As Immanuel Kant said, these are the voices you weigh—not number.

So take that vision, put feet under it, and run with it. If you do, you'll have a great start to realizing new levels of achievement.

EVALUATE

The name of the game in business today is quality assessment. Big budgets and even significant numbers of personnel are involved. Everyone is quality conscious.

Philip Crosby in his classic book, *Let's Talk Quality,* tells of a dinner speech he once made. In the speech he talked about the percentage of mice droppings allowed in wheat by industry standards. He said that he had checked the wheat in their dinner rolls and found that there were less mouse droppings than allowed by law, so he had the chef add more to reach the quota. As his listeners looked at their rolls, they graphically got his point—quality isn't about the minimum we can do and still get by. Businesses have traditionally accepted errors—1 percent, 5 percent. But in the church, where we emphasize perfection in our theology, we're satisfied with a 40 percent attrition rate. That's pitiful.

The Bible says, "Wisdom is better than weapons of war, but one bungler destroys much good." (Ecclesiastes 9:18, NRSV) Regarding evaluation, George W. Bush said, "If you aren't keeping record, then you're only practicing." Only the person who has already predetermined that he is a failure is afraid of evaluation. What is respected is inspected.

Albert Einstein observed, "The significant problems we face cannot be solved at the same level of thinking we were at when we created them." Therefore, retreats, planning seminars, and evaluation processes are helpful.

We must be serious about evaluating ourselves and our church. If business in the world can't go on as usual, certainly business in the church shouldn't either.

So I D.A.R.E. you to begin living, working, and ministering like the Lord is coming back soon. Begin to dream again—unlike goals, dreams are not limited by what you are certain you can achieve. Dreams, unlike goals, are often intangible. Martin Luther King said, "I have a dream"; he didn't say, "I have a strategic plan." He didn't manage his movement . . .

- He dreamed it.
- He articulated it.
- He realized it.
- He evaluated it.

Consider Pete Seibert's story. A ski instructor and former ski trooper in World War II, Siebert had wanted nothing more since the age of twelve than to start a ski area. One day, after an exhausting seven-hour climb in deep snow, he reached the summit of a mountain in the Gore Range in Colorado. Staring down at the vast bowls below and at the stunning peaks beyond, Seibert said to himself, "This is as good as any mountain I've seen."

Compared to the hard work that followed, the seven-hour trek was like a leisurely stroll. Seibert had to climb mountains of red tape, meet the U.S. Forest Service's stiff leasing requirements, and raise large amounts of capital "from frugal friends and suspicious strangers" in order to buy land from ranchers and build a village.

Almost everyone thought he was crazy, but Seibert and his group thought they could do anything they wanted. Seibert's dream became Vail, Colorado.

Through one of the greatest visionaries of all time, God said, "Higher than the highest human thought can reach is God's ideal for His children" (Ellen G. White, *Education,* p. 18).

I D.A.R.E. you to dream those dreams, to articulate the vision in a new way as you realize what God has called you to do. And then to evaluate that vision and those dreams periodically to be sure you're being all that you can be by God's power.

Then, as God works through you, begin to realize those dreams in your community of believers and among those not yet of the body of faith. And continually evaluate what you are doing and where you are headed. If you do this, by God's grace and power, you and your organization will exponentially transcend any past accomplishments and obtain that quintessential level God has ordained for you.

That's my dream!

"Everything requires time. It is the one truly unusual condition. Yet most people take for granted this unique, irreplaceable, and necessary resource. Nothing else, perhaps, distinguishes effective executives as much as their tender loving care of time."
—*Peter Drucker.*

"If every moment were valued and rightly employed, we should have time for everything that we need to do for ourselves or for the world."
—*Ellen G. White, The Ministry of Healing,* page 208.

CHAPTER 5

TIME ENOUGH

According to one survey, top American business executives spend fifty to sixty hours per week on the job. A poll of clergy reported that they spend seventy to eighty hours each week. In one church, members were asked to indicate the amount of time they expected their pastor to spend in administration, budget, community outreach, visiting, sermon preparation, etc. The average totaled eighty-two hours a week. One saint expected her pastor to work 200 hours per week, although there are only 168 hours in a week! Actually, that is significant because it demonstrates the fact that expectations are often greater than reality allows.

But if leaders succumb to unrealistic expectations, they will become frustrated, nervous, and uptight. Or as one harried executive said to his secretary, "Where did I put my pencil?"

"Behind your ear," she replied.

"I'm a busy man," said the executive. "Don't you realize that? Which ear?"

PRIORITIZE

This brings us to an important point—leaders must have an "intentional" ministry. Time management expert, Edgar Mills, defines the concept of "intentionality" as: "Purposely directing one's life as much as possible rather than allowing it to be determined by external pressures." You have intentions, plans, goals, and objectives. You take a proactive posture as opposed to a reactionary one. In other words, as a leader, you have to proactively take charge of your schedule minute by minute.

Every intern has experienced the "gopher complex"—being told by the supervisor to go for this and go for that. I can hear some of you saying, "But my organization has grown accustomed to me doing these types of things." Then a simple equation comes into play: Education + negotiation = respect. Try it. It works.

LIST PRIORITIES

We've all heard that Martin Luther was supposed to have said, "I have so much to do today that I must spend four hours in prayer." Of Christ it was said, "No other life was ever so crowded with labor and responsibility as was that of Jesus; yet how often He was found in prayer!" (Ellen G. White, *The Desire of Ages,* p. 362). As one studies the biographies of great spiritual leaders down through the ages, they were often people of quality and quantity prayer. That's getting one's priorities right.

A second priority too often neglected by leaders is their own family. I well remember, as a young minister, traveling with an older, experienced leader who opened up his heart to me. He told me how his son had turned his back on God, left the church, and moved away from home. He went on to tell me with emotion that one time his son said to him, "Dad, you are a great leader, but you are one lousy dad." This great church leader whom I so much respected and who had made such an impact on so many other people, had lost his sense of priority, and in turn he had lost his son.

I determined as a young youth leader that by God's grace I would never give my children an excuse to say that their dad was a great leader, but a lousy dad.

Many years later when my own twenty-two-year-old son, Troy, was with me on a mission trip to Africa, we faced a life-threatening situation. We didn't know if we would survive. In the midst of that situation he put his hand on my shoulder and said, "Dad, if this is the end, I want you to know I'm ready." I've got to tell you that I fondly remember the hundreds of people we baptized on that mission trip but I cherish the memory of my own son's testimony even more.

It's been reported that American dads spend only thirty-seven seconds a day communicating with their children and only ten minutes a day with their spouse. One has to compare that with the amount of time and energy spent in later years worrying through sleepless nights about their wayward children. A little more enjoyable time, spent a little sooner, could prevent some agonizing time later.

A number of years ago, Dr. H. George Anderson in turning down the presidency of the Lutheran Church of America, said, "We could have worked out the details of the job, but the issue is how close I can be with my children in the next few years. They are not a responsibility; they are a joy to me. At this age, they start talking to you, sharing what they think, and I don't want to miss it."

SELF-IMPROVEMENT

Part of being an effective leader is to spend regular time in self-improvement. For Christian leaders that naturally includes the spiritual, but it also includes the physical and mental. A regular, daily exercise program could not only lengthen your productive years but their quality too.

And no leader is worth his salary if he isn't staying on the cutting edge professionally by reading, seminars, continuing education classes, etc.

There are also those who out of dedication or through insecurity have become workaholics. As one leader said, "The devil never takes a vacation, how can I?" Well, that may sound noble, but Christ, who carried a far greater burden than any of us, advocated that His disciples come apart to rest a while. Commenting on this, Ellen White, says, "It was their duty to rest" (*The Desire of Ages,* p. 360). As one wise person stated, "I can do a year's work in eleven months, but I can't do it in twelve months." As humans, we simply work more efficiently if we plan change into our schedule. I was amused by the story of a pastor who observed his hired hand idly sitting beside a team of horses as they took a much needed rest. "Shouldn't you be doing something worthwhile as the horses rest," remonstrated the pastor.

"Yes, sir! And the next time you go into the pulpit, Pastor, take a bushel of potatoes with you so you can peel them during the closing hymn!"

Horses and leaders need and deserve some regular rest.

PLAN AHEAD

You've heard the illustration of poor planning? A guy puts fifty cents into the coffee machine. Out comes the coffee, then cream, then sugar . . . and then the cup! How often we get things all backwards.

It's good to remember that Christ spent thirty years planning and preparing—and three years implementing. Yet we never see Christ harried or hurried.

It's interesting to note in your Bible concordance all the references to runners—Phillip, Elijah, Peter—but never Christ. He was deliberate and followed a previously developed plan.

Our church is a strong advocate of creationism, yet how often we act like evolutionists. We throw our programs together hurriedly and expect them to somehow just happen. And the end result is indeed chaos.

Pastors know that planning a new sermon every Sabbath can become a chore. Yet if the topics are prayerfully thought out well in advance, then ideas, illustrations, and key thoughts come during the natural course of everyday reading and communicating. It is easy to pick out a sermon that was prepared on Friday night. Conversely advance sermon preparation avoids repetition, pet themes, and can even save time in the end.

SHORT-TERM PLANNING

All time management experts will say that one of the most basic time savers is also one of the most simple. Make a list.

I believe in making lists. I've urged others to make lists in order to become more efficient and save time. But sometimes I still don't do it. However, I can personally attest to the fact that when I make a list in the morning—or even the night before—I start working on the most important or the most challenging items on that list, and don't get distracted until I've finished. I get more accomplished.

As you become more conscious of this principle, you will also appreciate the idea of making the best use of your prime time.

Charles Schwab made little-known Bethlehem Steel into the largest independent steel producer in the world. One secret of his success? A consultant told Schwab early in his career, "Write down the six most important things you have to do—and stay with them." In a few weeks, Schwab paid the consultant $25,000 for his advice. He had learned to focus on a few important things and get those done. Tom Peters, author of *In Search of Excellence,* said, "Every leader that makes things happen is a Mono Maniac."

Use prime time to tackle the toughies. One company had a policy that no major decisions would be made after 4:00 P.M. In the church, no committee or board meeting should run past 9:00 P.M.—certainly not after 10:00 P.M. That's when the devil takes the chair. Tackle the toughies during prime time.

THOSE SPARE MINUTES

Great leaders learn not to waste time. At twenty-six, William Carey pastored a small Baptist church, earning seventy-five dollars a year. He worked as a cobbler on the side to support his family, and he always kept a book beside his bench. In seven years he had learned five languages, including Greek and Hebrew. Before his death he supervised the translation of the Bible into forty languages—many of which he translated himself. One of the Strauss waltzes was written on the back of a menu while the composer was waiting for a meal. Harriet Beecher Stowe kept a pencil between her teeth while kneading dough. During breaks she would continue to write *Uncle Tom's Cabin*. One popular U.S. song was written while the composer was caught in a traffic jam.

Never say you don't have enough time. You have exactly the same number of hours per day that were given to Helen Keller, Pasteur, Michelangelo, Mother Teresa, Leonardo da Vinci, Thomas Jefferson, or Albert Einstein.

The adage is still true: Leaders are readers, and readers are leaders. Socrates said, "Employ your time in improving yourself by other men's writings; so you shall come easily by what others have labored hard for."

One time management expert says that a person can effectively read 50,000 words a minute. How? By deciding in one minute the book isn't worth reading! Be selective; always check the table of contents. And of course most of us spend hours driving to appointments which can be enhanced by listening to tapes.

DELEGATE

Every parent knows that it is often much easier to do a job yourself than to try to train a child to do it. However, the mark of a good leader is just that—to train those he is responsible to lead. Dwight D. Eisenhower's definition of leadership was, "The art of getting somebody to do something you want him to do because he wants to do it."

I well remember the first three-church district I pastored. I was young and enjoyed mowing the church lawn. And they would have let me do it as long as I was willing—along with washing the church windows and cleaning the bathrooms. One minister said, "I'll never do anything someone else can do." Another said, "When the office machine salesman delivered a new piece of equipment to the church office he offered to show me how to operate it. I promptly and politely showed him to the door."

Now the idea is not that a church leader is too good to do menial labor. Absolutely not. And in times of special need he or she should be ready and willing to pitch in and shovel the snow or sweep the walk. But not on a regular basis. A leader has skills and gifts that should be used for what he or she was trained to do. There are plenty of others who can't lead, but who are willing and able to fix the school bus or mow the church lawn . . . and incidentally do it better than you can.

A writer with unusual insights wrote, "Ministers should not do the work which belongs to the church, thus wearying themselves, and preventing others from performing their duty. They should teach the members how to labor in the church and in the community" (Ellen G. White, *Christian Service*, p. 69).

For all his foibles, former president Richard Nixon did know how to foster loyalty. He once wrote, "Both in the areas in which he is an expert and in those in which he is not, an effective leader must learn to delegate . . . he is hired for the big decisions, and he owes it to the country to delegate the small ones."

EVALUATE

Efficiency experts say we waste fifty percent of our time. Peter Drucker, one of the most respected writers on leadership, says, "In 10 percent of our time we accomplish 90 percent of our output. If that is so, we'd better critique and evaluate how we do business. One way to do that is to block off the day in fifteen minute segments and keep track. If you find yourself reading the newspaper thirty minutes, checking e-mail and chatting with your colleagues, you can quickly lose the prime time part of the day."

So do a personal inventory. You will probably realize that you need to make some radical changes. Put into practice the principles we've been discussing in these chapters. And remember what business tycoon J.C. Penney said, "If you've been doing it that way for twenty years, that in itself probably means it's wrong."

Paul said it even better, "Make the best use of your time, despite all the evils of these days" (Ephesians 5:16, Phillips). And speaking of the value of time, Ellen G. White wrote, "Every moment of time is fraught with eternal results" (*The Desire of Ages,* p. 91).

LET'S REVIEW

Here are some key points that time management experts advocate:

- Set priorities. Cultivate an intentional ministry.
- Plan ahead. Avoid the panic.
- Delegate—to church members, spouse, youth. Remember what one leader said, "I'll never do anything someone else can do."
- Make lists either the night before or in the morning.
- Work in blocks.
- Remember prime time when 10 percent of your time can accomplish 90 percent of your output.
- Handle work only once. (For example, respond to letters when you read them the first time.)
- Be a minute minder—read while waiting; dictate in your car.
- Relax. You can't get a year's work done in twelve months, but you probably can in eleven.
- Have a procrastination drawer. This is risky, but valid. Some things will take care of themselves.
- Learn to say "No."
- Discard it. When in doubt, throw it out.
- Parkinson's law. "Any job tends to expand to fill the time allotted."

- Kill it. Robert Townsend who wrote *Up the Organization*, says, "Every company should have a vice president in charge of killing things."
- Get up and get going. Benjamin Franklin advised, "Plow deep while sluggards sleep." Aristotle Onassis and billionaire John D. Rockefeller both limited themselves to a few hours of sleep per night and were up at 5 A.M. Pope Leo XIII was able to be vigorous and productive on three hours' sleep per night. Ellen White often worked and prayed much of the night. Someone said to George Muller, "Pray for me that I can get up earlier." To which he responded, "You get one leg out, and I'll pray that the Lord will help you get the other one out."
- Evaluate. Always ask of any job, "Is it worth the amount of life it will cost?"
- Ask God for help. His commands are His enablings.

In a university commencement address several years ago, Brian Dyson, CEO of Coca Cola Enterprises, spoke of the relation of work to one's other commitments:

Imagine life as a game in which you are juggling some five balls in the air. You name them "work," "family," "health," "friends," and "spirit"—and you're keeping all of these in the air. You will soon understand that work is a rubber ball. If you drop it, it will bounce back. But the other four balls— "family," "friends," "health," and "spirit"—are made of glass. If you drop one of these, they will be irrevocably scuffed, marked, nicked, damaged or even shattered. They will never be the same. You must understand that and strive for balance in your life.

Don't use time or words carelessly. Neither can be retrieved. Life is not a race, but a journey to be savored each step of the way. Yesterday is history, tomorrow is a mystery and today is a gift. That's why we call it "the present."

To Realize . . .
To realize the value of one year ask a student who has failed a final exam.
To realize the value of one month ask a mother who has given birth to a premature baby.
To realize the value of one week ask an editor of a weekly newspaper.
To realize the value of one hour ask the lovers who are waiting to meet.
To realize the value of one minute ask the person who has missed the train, bus, or plane.
To realize the value of one second ask a person who has survived an accident.
To realize the value of one millisecond ask the person who has won a silver medal in the Olympics.
Time waits for no one. Treasure every moment you have.

"While many believe that seeing is believing,
others of us know that believing is seeing."
—*Anonymous.*

"Don't be afraid to take a big step if one is indicated.
You can't cross a chasm in two small jumps."
—*David Lloyd George.*

CHAPTER 6

WE'VE GOT THE ROCK

One of the most familiar stories in the Bible is also one that is worth repeating in the context of our responsibilities as church leaders. The story involves two confident individuals facing each other across the Valley of Elah and thousands of faint-hearted wimps watching with great interest.

Of the two main players, one is considerably more prominent. Goliath—a big, bellowing, blustering, blasphemous behemoth, the original Big Foot. Of course, it's easy for me to say that about an obnoxious, terror-inflicting giant who lived so long ago and far away! It's always easier to be courageous after the fact. But it's much different when you are facing a giant eyeball to kneecap!

And Goliath was big—maybe over ten feet tall in his smelly bare feet. That's big even by NBA standards! And as if his size didn't evoke sufficient fear, he wore a coat of bronze that weighed two hundred pounds complete with a bronze helmet and a solid iron spear the tip of which weighed fifteen pounds.

Two times a day he came out to taunt the enemy much to the glee of his comrades. I can still remember those haunting words on the old 33 1/3 rpm *Bible Story* records I played over and over as a little boy. "Am I a dog that you come to me with a stick? I will give your flesh to the birds of the air and the beasts of the field."

As Goliath stood there on the plain, haughty and raucous, he seemed so imposing as to actually blot out the Sun—S-O-N, that is. And each boast brought from his enemies the desired response—a silent holding of the breath with only the sound of their knees knocking together in cadence betraying their abject fear.

This had been going on for forty horrendously humbling days with Goliath's buddies reveling in the sport. The Israelites on the other hand were exhausted from sleepless nights and traumatic days, similar to a group of condemned prisoners on death row awaiting the inevitable.

It was to this dispirited, disgruntled, and disheartened group that young David came, bringing with him a basket of—can you believe it?—bread and cheese! Can't you just imagine the response from his older brothers?

Now a lesser boy would have dropped off his basket and fearfully fled for home. And in reality, David did have a rather undistinguished past. Seemingly, no one had ever taken him seriously. Even Samuel thought he should anoint David's older brother to be king; everyone had all but forgotten about the shepherd boy with the unspectacular past.

But David had something Goliath didn't have. Something all the children of Israel didn't have. Something that even his own brothers didn't have.

David had the rock!

If I had been David, I would have thought like Saul. Let's at least improve the odds by getting state-of-the-art military weaponry and a suit of armor. In fact I would want a tank or maybe one of those smart missiles that can hit the door knob on an enemy's building or an F-16. Certainly something more than just a rock.

But that's what David had—his rock.

Today we hear a lot about rocks:

- Trucks built like a rock.
- Music that rocks.
- Insurance as dependable as a rock.
- Hard Rock Cafes from New York to London.

But David's rock was different. Was it because it was perfect? No. It may have even had some rough edges. Isn't it amazing how God will so often use imperfect instruments—imperfect organizations, imperfect leaders, imperfect members—to bring glory to Him?

So David had the rock. As is so often the case in the Bible, there is a symbol here. David's imperfect rock represents the perfect Rock—Jesus Christ. Like the imperfect cornerstone later in his son Solomon's temple, the imperfect rock represented the perfect Rock. So young David's five small, imperfect rocks represented the true Rock of Ages.

You see, this isn't about great big Goliath and poor little David. This is about a great big God and poor little Goliath. The Bible says:

"You come against me with sword and spear and javelin, but I come against you in the name of the Lord Almighty. . . whom you have defied. This day the Lord will hand you over to me, and I'll strike you down and cut off your head . . . for the battle is the Lord's" (1 Samuel 17:45- 47, NIV).

Wow! That's pretty confident for a young, inexperienced boy with only a few rocks for a weapon.

> As the Philistine moved closer to attack him, David ran quickly toward the battle line to meet him [notice it says "toward," not "from"]. Reaching into his bag and taking out a stone, he slung it and struck the Philistine on the forehead. The stone sank into his forehead, and he fell facedown on the ground. So David triumphed over the Philistine . . . without a sword . . . he struck down the Philistine and killed him. David ran and stood over him. He took hold of the Philistine's sword. . . . After he killed him, he cut off his head with the sword (1 Samuel 17:48-51, NIV).

And the rest is history. What a great story of encouragement and challenge! David had faith, vision, and commitment—and most importantly, David had the Rock!

And with that Rock he could face not only the giant Goliath, he could face any giant, no matter how big, no matter how mean, no matter how ugly!

The apostle Paul knew the reality underlying success. He says in Romans 9:33 (quoting, actually, Isaiah 8:14), "See, I lay in Zion a . . . rock that makes them fall" (NIV).

The bad news is that the giants keep coming. According to 2 Samuel 21 even after David defeated Goliath he faced other giants (and some of them weren't two legged). He faced the giants of hot-blooded lust and cold-blooded murder and failed his God. But the good news is that when David relied on his Rock, he was always successful.

Are you facing giants today? Personal problems that seem overpowering, threatening, impossible? Or perhaps the giants of:

- Betrayal.
- Discouragement.
- Conflict.
- Finances.
- Sickness.
- Broken relationships.
- Loss of a loved one.

I have good news for you—we've got the Rock! Does this seem too philosophical? Too nebulous? Too ethereal?

No! Church leader, you've got the Rock. And there's nothing more solid and dependable than the Rock. Let me share just one classic illustration.

It happened to a small Adventist Church in the foothills of the Great Smoky Mountains. They had built a new sanctuary on a piece of land given by a church member. Ten days before the opening of the new church the county inspectors informed the pastor that the parking lot was too small for the size of the building. Until the parking lot was expanded, they would be unable to use the new sanctuary.

The problem was the congregation had used every bit of land except for the mountain against which the church had been built. In order to build more parking spaces they would literally have to move the mountain out of the backyard.

These members faced a foreboding giant of a problem.

Undaunted the pastor announced that the next weekend he would meet with all of the members who had "mountain-moving faith." They would have a prayer meeting petitioning God to move the mountain out of the backyard and somehow have the space paved and painted before the grand opening.

Only two dozen of the hundred members gathered for prayer. They prayed for three hours. At 10:00 P.M. the pastor said the final amen. "We'll open next Sabbath as scheduled," he said. "God (the dependable Rock of Ages) has never let us down before. I believe He will be faithful this time too."

The next morning as the pastor was working in his study there came a loud knocking on the door. When he called "Come in," a rough-looking construction foreman appeared, took off his hard hat, and entered.

"Pardon me, pastor. I'm from the Acme Construction Company over in the next county. We're building a large new shopping mall over there, and we need some fill dirt. Would you be willing to sell us a piece of that mountain behind the church? We'll pay you for the dirt, haul it away, and then repave all the exposed areas free of charge. But there is one condition—we need to have it right away. We can't proceed until we get the dirt in and allow it to settle properly."

The little church was dedicated the next weekend as originally scheduled. The pastor reported that there were considerably more members with mountain-moving, giant-felling faith on opening day than there had been the previous week at prayer meeting!

Some people believe faith comes from miracles. Others know miracles come from faith. Some think seeing is believing. Others know that believing is seeing.

David believed he would see miracles because he had the Rock. His brothers became believers, and so did their comrades.

Today in the church family we face some giants, too, that need to fall. And I am here to tell you that we have the Rock! Back in your conference, your church, your organization, your members, your family, you have the Rock!

As we go forward to do God's business, we may seem inadequate as individuals—even unspectacular at times. But remember: We have the Rock! As you lay down this book and go back to your office, you may face a giant standing in your way. Put a smile on your face and say, "It's OK, I've got the Rock!"

"At a gut level, all of us know that much more goes into the process of keeping a large organization vital and responsive than the policy statements, new strategies, plans, budgets, and organization charts can possibly depict…. If we want change, we fiddle with the strategy. Or we change the structure. Perhaps the time has come to change our ways."
—*Peters and Waterman, In Search of Excellence.*

"We tend to meet any situation by reorganization, and a wonderful method it can be for creating the illusion of progress while producing confusion, inefficiency, and demoralization."
—*Petrinius Arbiter, 210 B.C.*

"Commitment isn't enough anymore. You also have to have professionalism or you're going to go out of business."
—*John R. Garrison, president, National Easter Seal Society.*

CHAPTER 7

THE P. T. BARNUM SYNDROME

Phineas Taylor Barnum had a dream. That dream led to the establishment in 1870 of arguably the "greatest show on earth." Barnum is still known today as the co-founder of Barnum and Bailey's circus. Barnum built his fortune on a rather unflattering philosophy, which he articulated as, "There's a sucker born every minute."

I want to suggest that sometimes we church leaders subconsciously operate as though we believe Barnum's theory. Let's be honest. If, in fact, the primary purpose or superordinate goal, as psychologists call it, is to reveal the character of God in such a way that people commit themselves to Jesus, then maybe we'd better start asking ourselves some questions.

As a starter, ask yourself: "How many people accepted Jesus Christ as their Savior last year because of what I did personally through the power of the Holy Spirit?"

"Oh, but I preached fifty great sermons last year," someone says. Wonderful! But, "How many people accepted Jesus Christ as their Savior because of what you did?"

"But I traveled 50,000 miles." Yes, but "How many . . .?"

"But I sat on a hundred committees, many of which I chaired." OK, but "How many . . .?"

"But we had a great school year with a 5 percent increase in enrollment." That's great! But, "How many . . .?"

"But our summer camp and our Pathfinder club had the largest attendance ever." Terrific! But, "How many . . .?"

You see, we're all busy—probably too busy—preaching, promoting, traveling, attending meetings. But why? For what? Who in the world is responsible for the bottom line if it's not me and it's not you? And for our church, the bottom line is souls accepting Christ as their Savior.

It appears we believe that if we just work hard enough and long enough, travel enough and stay busy long enough, maybe send out enough brochures or even have enough people enroll in a Bible course, that miraculously we'll experience results. As Barnum would say, "Some sucker will bite."

Could the majority of our efforts be going into greasing the machinery—keeping the organization running efficiently? One administrator humorously reported,

> When our PC's are all turned on, we have what is known as "email hour." During this period everyone sends email to everyone else. If you happen to have nothing in particular to email about, you email someone, saying that you have nothing to report. This gives a stimulating exchange of ideas and helps build camaraderie during the first hour of the day which otherwise could be wasted on less profitable pursuits.

Our church and most of its entities tend to be rather magnificent organizational machines that run quite efficiently for the most part. The principles outlined by God for this church still keep us functioning. But could the majority of our efforts be going into scratching our own backs? There's no risk, no pain, everybody feels good, happy and contented . . . and sends more emails.

Let me overstate my case to make a point. Let me facetiously suggest that we print our own SDA money. We would no longer need any federal currency. Here's how it would work.

Sam David Anderson (SDA) works at an industry owned by an Adventist. When he gets paid he gets his salary in Adventist dollars. After tithe and offerings, he begins spending his Adventist money. His children naturally attend an Adventist school so he pays their tuition in Adventist currency. Sammy, Jr. broke his arm, but since there is an Adventist hospital nearby, that's no problem. And when Susie needed a dentist there were plenty of Adventist dentists willing to accept his SDA cash.

Since Sam lives in an Adventist center, there is also an Adventist health food store for buying groceries. Wanting a newly published book he stops by the ABC. While there he sees a new CD that he heard while listening to the local Adventist radio station.

And so it goes—from appliances to car dealers, tailors to hair dressers, wood stoves to well drillers. Everything Sam and his family needs he can get at a bargain from an SDA business using his Adventist dollars. When Sam finally gets home and has eaten his veggie delight, he sits down and watches, what else, but 3ABN!

So those Adventist bucks could circulate entirely within Adventist circles without one red cent getting into the hands of the "Gentiles." There might even be some additional advantages—like circumventing the decree that no one can buy or sell during the time of trouble!

Obviously, I'm grossly overstating my case to make the point. But seriously, as a church we can be guilty of going through the motions—turning all the right wheels, talking to ourselves, scratching our own backs, and, yes, sending lots of emails. And in reality that might be very efficient, but it wouldn't be very effective.

How can we change this monster of a bureaucracy that we have become into a responsive and responsible organization? Someone said it's like kicking a dinosaur in January and hearing it grunt in July. It won't be easy, and it certainly won't be fast.

PLAN TO SUCCEED

For a church that strongly believes in creation, we often throw our programs together like evolutionists. Have you ever heard a leader say, "I don't want to restrict the Holy Spirit by planning too far in advance"? Or, "I don't prepare my sermon until Friday night so that I can speak to current needs"? My response is: Since when can't the Holy Spirit see well into the future? Christ's parable of the farmer in Matthew 13 is a good example. The farmer not only planted—not only broadcast the seed—he planned to reap too.

HAVE GOALS

Seneca said, "If a man knows not what harbor he seeks, any wind is the right wind." Most leaders will tell you they have goals, but to be worth anything those goals have to be carefully outlined. A good measurement of a goal is how well it fits the acronym SAM—specific, attainable, measurable.

Specific: To plan to share the gospel is nice, but to strategize having two more evangelistic series than last year is being specific.

Attainable: To set a goal that you know you'll reach automatically is not leadership. Conversely, to set unrealistic goals is discouraging. So good leaders have "stretch" goals that can be reached with efficient work and significant prayer.

Measurable: To plan to have an increase in baptisms is a worthy goal, but to set a goal of having 10 percent more baptisms than last year is measurable, and you'll know if you reach it.

Incidentally, there are those who will always be critical about numbers, particularly in the area of baptisms. Of course it is possible to overdo numerical goals. But baptismal numbers or any other numbers that represent people are important. It is interesting to me that when the disciples went fishing John records that they brought in 153 large fish. Now that's about as specific as one can get.

In other words, what we value we measure.

MENTORING

A rule of good management is that everyone should have a mentor and be a mentor. Generally, as a beginning worker, we don't have a choice of whether or not we want to have a mentor. Some of these mentors are better than others, but I tell pastoral interns, "You will always learn from your senior pastor. Some of it you'll want to emulate. Some of it you'll definitely not want to repeat, but it is all learning." That's the role of a mentor. And it's usually not optional to have one.

However, being a mentor is by choice. And the leader who is unwilling or unable to take the time or demonstrate the patience to mentor a younger worker is neglecting one of his or her most important God-given roles. Generally the reason for this reluctance is either a lack of knowledge or insecurity; we're afraid that we might be shown up by someone who can do the job as well or better than we can and that we won't be needed.

Moses is a wonderful example of the principle of mentoring. As leaders we would do well to study his life as an example for us. Moses was challenged by "the greatest work ever given to man" (Ellen G. White, *Patriarchs and Prophets,* p. 255). With the exception of Jesus, Moses may have been the greatest leader to walk this earth. "As historian, poet, philosopher, general of armies, and legislator, he stands without a peer" (Ibid., p. 246).

Dr. Danny Kellum, headmaster of Donelson Christian Academy, wrote about what he called one of the greatest mathematical problems in the world:

> Moses and the people were in the desert, but what was he going to do with them? They had to be fed, and feeding three or 3.5 million people requires a lot of food.
>
> According to the Quartermaster General in the Army, it is reported that Moses would have to have 1,500 tons of food each day. Do you know that to bring that much food each day, two freight trains each a mile long would be required!
>
> Besides you must remember, they were out in the desert, and they would have to have firewood to use in cooking the food. This would take 4,000 tons of wood and a few more freight trains each a mile long, just for one day.
>
> And just think, they were forty years in transit.
>
> Oh, yes, they would have to have water. If they only had enough to drink and wash a few dishes, it would take thousands of gallons each day, and another long freight train with tank cars just to bring water!
>
> And then another thing. They had to get across the Red Sea at night. Now, if they went on a narrow path, double file, the line would be 800 miles long and would require thirty-

five days and nights to get through. So, there had to be a space in the Red Sea, three miles wide so that they could walk 5,000 abreast to get over in one night.

But then another problem. Each time they camped at the end of the day, they needed a campground, or a total of several square miles, think of it! This space just for nightly camping.

Do you think Moses figured all this out before he left Egypt? If you do, think again. I think not! You see, Moses believed in God. God took care of these things for him.

Do you think God can take care of all your needs too?

Well, I can't vouch for all those statistics, but the point is obvious.

You recall the story. This great leader was, like most leaders, overworked. His wife, Zipporah, was beginning to react to his priorities—or lack thereof—and complained to her father, Jethro. So Jethro did a little mentoring. It is interesting to note that Moses accepted Jethro's counsel.

The Lord had greatly honored Moses, and had wrought wonders by his hand; but the fact that he had been chosen to instruct others did not lead him to conclude that he himself needed no instruction. The chosen leader of Israel listened gladly to the suggestions of the godly priest of Midian, and adopted his plan as a wise arrangement (Ellen G. White, *Patriarchs and Prophets,* p. 301).

You see, like too many twenty-first-century leaders, Moses was so conscientious that it was about to kill him and ruin his family.

He was trying to carry all the responsibilities of leadership on his own shoulders. He needed to delegate some of his duties to others. God was leading Moses, but nonetheless he could not humanly bear the burdens of leadership alone for forty years. Until Jethro came along, this is what Moses' management chart looked like.

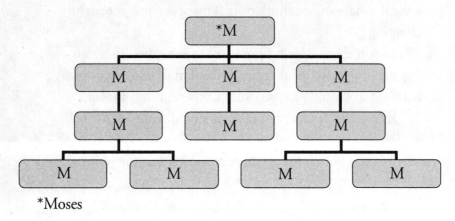

*Moses

That's right. Moses did it all—from CEO to sanitation engineer. But God used his wife (a good lesson in listening to our spouses) who talked to Jethro who mentored Moses. And Moses then became a successful mentor for Joshua himself. Did it pay off? You bet. The Bible tells us that at age 120 Moses' "eyes were not weak nor his strength gone" (Deuteronomy 34:7, NIV).

ACCOUNTABILITY

Finally we need to evaluate, check, assess, and become accountable. Someone described the process of nonaccountability like this: The early Christians were accountable to Jesus. Then the Catholics came along and said they were accountable to a priest. Then Protestants came along and taught that all the believers were accountable to each other. And finally by the time psychologist Sigmund Freud came along, no one was accountable to anyone!

Well there has been a tendency in recent years to resist accountability. If the truth were known it goes back to Cain who said, "Am I my brother's keeper?"

As a leader, I've learned that only those who have already determined they are not successful are afraid of accountability. Champion athletes, particularly Olympic champions, are always being evaluated, timed, measured, and in recent years, videoed and analyzed. Someone said, "Feedback is the breakfast of champions." But people don't naturally like to be evaluated.

Socrates said, "An unexamined life is not worth living." President George W. Bush said, "If you're not keeping record, then you're only practicing." And J. C. Penney of department store fame, said, "If we've been doing the same thing the same way for twenty years, that in itself probably means it's wrong." But we never know unless we evaluate.

So these three principles of good leadership—goal setting, delegating, and accountability are timeless. In fact while they are found in the latest management theory books they are also found in the Bible. Did you know that? Yes, all the way through, in fact. "The Lord God took the man and put him in the Garden of Eden to work it and take care of it" (Genesis 2:15, NIV). That's goal setting. "And the Lord God commanded the man . . ." (verse 16, NIV). That's delegating. "You are free to eat from any tree in the garden; but you must not eat from the tree of the knowledge of good and evil, for when you eat of it you will surely die" (verses 16, 17, NIV). That's evaluating or accountability. Then in Revelation 22:17-20 the Bible says, "The Spirit and the bride say, 'Come!' [goal setting] And let him who hears say, 'Come!' Whoever is thirsty, let him come; and whoever wishes, let him take the free gift of the water of life [delegating]. I warn everyone who hears the words of the prophecy of this book: If anyone adds anything to them, God will add to him the plagues described in this book. And if anyone takes words away from this book of prophecy, God will take away from him his share in the tree of life and in the holy city, which are described in this book. He who testifies to these things says, 'Yes, I am coming soon' [evaluating or accountability]" (NIV).

When the Lord comes He's going to want to know that His leaders have not been operating under the Barnum Syndrome. When He pronounces the words, "Well done good and faithful servant," it will not be pronounced merely because of our efficiency, but also because of our effectiveness.

"It is better to aim your spear at the moon and hit an eagle than to aim at the eagle and hit a rock."
—*etched on a California building.*

"Give us men to match our mountains."
—*Anonymous.*

CHAPTER 8

THE SKY'S THE LIMIT

I remember attending the Sligo Adventist Church in Takoma Park, Maryland as a small boy. The pastor was Taylor G. Bunch, a great and respected pulpiteer. I remember one Sabbath he said to the congregation, "Some of you may not appreciate me as your pastor, but someday I'll leave this church, and you'll get a new pastor, and maybe he'll be from your tribe. And then you'll be more happy." I don't know what prompted that declaration—possibly some of his saints were grumbling about his preaching—but that was my introduction to the concept of different tribes.

John the revelator talks about the tribes in Revelation:

> After this I looked and there before me was a great multi-tude that no one could count, from every nation, tribe, people and language, standing before the throne and in front of the Lamb. They were wearing white robes and were hold-ing palm branches in their hands. And they cried out in a loud voice: "Salvation belongs to our God, who sits on the throne, and to the Lamb" (Revelation 7:9, 10, NIV).

Today sociologists would probably refer to these "tribes" John talks about as "people groups." The key word in this passage, however, is "multitude." I'd like to suggest that we church leaders have tradition-ally thought too small. Psychologists call it "sectarian paranoia." We've emphasized that only eight were saved in the ark. Only Lot's family, minus one, were saved out of Sodom. Only 7,000 had not bowed the knee to Baal during Elijah's time. Just five virgins were ready to attend the wedding. There are only 144,000 redeemed saints brought to view in Revelation (which incidentally caused quite a discussion when our early Adventist Church exceeded that number of members). Then there was the "little flock" and of course the remnant.

But looking down to the twenty-first century, John sees a "mul-titude" too great to number. What that says to me, as a leader, is that if we're going to realize that prophecy in our time it will necessitate some changes in thinking.

- We'll need to get beyond our conventional wisdom.
- We'll need to get beyond traditional methods.
- We'll need to get beyond management by comparison.

Do you know what I'm talking about when I say "management by comparison"? We're all guilty of it. If you're a pastor, you com-pare your number of baptisms to the other churches in the confer-ence. If you're an academy administrator, you compare your enroll-ment gain each September with the other academies in the union. If you're in the conference office, you compare your tithe gain to the other conferences in the union. And on and on. And then we joke that if the indicators are up, it's obviously because of good leadership. If they are down, it must be the economy. And we rationalize until we can feel quite smug.

But I'm beginning to see that God expects something more. Through John, He's talking about a great "multitude" out there who will respond to the gospel. But He needs leaders who are big thinkers—bona fide change agents, paradigm shifters, leaders who aren't satisfied with the status quo.

Robert Kennedy paraphrased George Bernard Shaw when he said, "There are some people who look at the way things are and ask 'Why?'; there are others who look at the way things could be and ask 'Why not?' "

You and I had better stop asking "Why?" and start asking, "Why not?" Or are we like Martin Van Buren, governor of New York, who on January 31, 1829, wrote President Jackson the following letter:

> The canal system of this country is being threatened by the spread of a new form of transportation known as "railroads." The federal government must preserve the canals for the following reasons:
>
> 1. If canal boats are supplanted by railroads, serious unemployment will result. Captains, cooks, drivers, hostlers, repairmen, and lock tenders will be left without means of livelihood, not to mention the numerous farmers now employed in growing hay for horses.
>
> 2. Boat builders would suffer, and towline, whip, and harness makers would be left destitute.
>
> 3. Canal boats are absolutely essential to the defense of the United States. In the event of the expected trouble with England, the Erie Canal would be the only means by which we could ever move the supplies so vital to waging modern war.

As you may well know, Mr. President, railroad carriages are pulled at the enormous speed of fifteen miles per hour by engines which, in addition to endangering life and limb of passengers, roar and snort their way through the countryside, setting fire to crops, scaring the livestock, and frightening women and children. The Almighty certainly never intended that people should travel at such breakneck speed.

Have you ever had any employees like Martin Van Buren? Have you ever personally acted like him? In his book, *If It Ain't Broke . . . Break It!* Robert J. Kriegle tells how he had the participants in a Hewlett Packard management training program choose areas in which they wanted to see things change. He then had them rank their projects from one to ten on a "passion index," with ten being "burning desire" and one being "smoldering ashes."

If their passion was below a seven, he told them to either get fired up or forget it. It's too tough out there, he said, to be wasting your time on something you're not fired up about. That's not bad counsel for church leaders as well.

You see, fire in the heart, passion, and dreams have a crucial role in differentiating the outstanding from the good:

- A recent nationwide industry study found that the most significant factor, the one that distinguished the "top" sales performers from the "good" (and in one sense all leaders are salesmen) was enthusiasm.
- TV sports analyst, John Madden, the former Super Bowl winning coach, says the difference between the guys who make the Pro Bowl and those who don't is enthusiasm.

- "If you don't have enthusiasm," Kemmons Wilson, Sr., founder of one of America's top hotel chains says, "you don't have anything."

Enthusiasm is an old word whose root meaning is "infused with spirit." Or as the Bible says, "For the children of this world are more astute in dealing with their own kind than are the children of light" (Luke 16:8, *The Jerusalem Bible*). You see, fire in the heart, passion, enthusiasm—these all have a crucial role in moving something from being merely "good" to being "outstanding."

It has been said many times, "He who aims at nothing is sure to hit it." Let's stop being consensus builders and managers and status quo bureaucrats. Let's be leaders. In other words let's start fulfilling prophecy.

So back to where we started. Multitudes will join the armies of the Lord.

> Many . . . will be seen hurrying hither and thither, constrained by the Spirit of God to bring the light to others. The truth, the Word of God, is as a fire in their bones, filling them with a burning desire to enlighten those who sit in darkness. Many, even among the uneducated, now proclaim the words of the Lord. Children are impelled by the Spirit to go forth and declare the message from heaven. The Spirit is poured out upon all who will yield to its promptings, and, casting off all man's machinery, his binding rules and cautious methods, they will declare the truth with the might of the Spirit's power. Multitudes will receive the faith and join the armies of the Lord (Ellen G. White, *Evangelism*, p. 700).

When athletes face the consummate test of the Olympics, they talk about how they must "take it to another level." So the next time somebody says, "The sky's the limit," I hope you'll say, "Oh no, not anymore. We broke that barrier with satellite evangelism. Now God is the only limit, and He has no limits."

I'm ready for the multitude to join the army of the Lord. How about you?

"If you want to know what it feels like to be a leader, put on a deerskin jacket and take a walk in the woods during hunting season."
—*Anonymous.*

"A smooth sea never made a skillful sailor."
—*Anonymous.*

"You don't need to look out the window. When you start getting the flak it means you're over the target."
—*Air Force bombadier.*

CHAPTER 9

AFTER THE LICKIN' . . . WE'RE STILL TICKIN'

Cotton Fitzsimmons at one time was the coach of the Atlanta Hawks basketball team. At that time it was the worst team in the National Basketball Association. Meeting with his team in the locker room just before another game, he said to the players, "Tonight I want you to think positive. I want you to:

- "Act like the best team in the NBA instead of the worst.
- "Act like we have a three-game winning streak instead of a three-game losing streak.
- "Act like this is the championship game, not just a regular game."

So they did. They went out with a positive attitude. They played the Boston Celtics, and guess what? They got whipped!

Coach Fitzsimmons was distraught until one of players patted him on the back and said, "It's OK, coach, just act like we won."

This is the New Age era of the self-help gurus, each getting rich on the philosophy of "What the mind can conceive, the body can achieve."

But I have news for them. These guys aren't church leaders!

Any church leader worth his salt will tell you that all the pep talks, all the positive thinking, sometimes even all the prayer in the world, doesn't counteract the fact that we leaders take some real beatings.

I'd like to suggest four keys to successfully coping with criticism that I've learned over the years, even if I haven't always practiced them.

1. Before you reject the criticism outright, be certain it's undeserved.

The apostle Peter said, "For what glory is it if you endure suffering when you are doing wrong?" (see 1 Peter 2:20).

Just because we work for an all-wise God doesn't make us omnipotent. The facts are that some criticism is deserved. As hard as I try, I don't do everything right. You and I can't be making scores of decisions each day and do them all right. I can save myself a lot of grief and pain and incidentally, considerable credibility, by admitting I've made a mistake—not in a patronizing, condescending way—but sincerely, saying, "Sorry, folks, I goofed," rather than making excuses or blaming someone else.

A coach was flabbergasted by a rookie who dropped a fly ball. Another ball went through his legs. The coach grabbed the glove and said, "I'll show you." The next line drive came to the coach. He stumbled, fell, and dropped the ball. "See," he said, "you messed up the field so bad no one can play in it."

2. Learn from the legitimate criticisms.

Someone said, "The smooth sea never made a skillful sailor." Stephen Neill said it another way, "Criticism is the manure in which the servants of the Lord grow best."

Georges Clemenceau once said, "I only read articles attacking me—never those that praise. They are too dangerous." Now personally I am still just human enough to enjoy being appreciated; but he has a point.

Having said that, it should challenge us as leaders to take the high road. Be a model worth emulating. I remember dealing with a controversial issue when I was a conference president. Afterwards, one saint came up and said to me, "I'll stick with you." I thanked him and said, "Even better you ought to stick with Christ." But the facts are that people do want to stick with their leaders if they are worth following.

3. Support each other.

Someone said, "You better stop criticizing your wife's judgment—after all, she married you!" Someone else quipped, "People who complain that the boss is dumb would be out of a job if he were any smarter."

The same principle is true for church leaders. You can't afford to criticize the organization—any part of it. After all, it chose to employ you!

So let's be in a mode of support. Cultivate the spiritual gift of support. You know how good it feels when you receive a card or letter expressing appreciation for something you did. What if each of us sent just one appreciation note a week to a colleague?

4. Learn to laugh at yourself.

No matter how good you are you're going to make mistakes. No matter how many home runs you hit sometimes you'll strike out. Babe Ruth, arguably the greatest home run hitter in baseball, struck out 488 times.

So do yourself and others a favor and don't take yourself too seriously. When you do something dumb, laugh it off. People will respect you much more than if you get all flustered and upset.

A former hockey coach of the Vancouver Canucks gave this explanation for being fired. "We were losing at home, and we weren't winning on the road. My failure as a coach was that I couldn't find any place else to play!"

You've got to know that people respect a leader that can admit their shortcomings, laugh at themselves, and move on.

5. We're not working for the perks.

Someone has said that when we work for the Lord, the pay isn't always that great, but the retirement plan is out of this world! There's a lot of truth to that. Most professional church leaders I've met aren't doing their job for the pay. And if that is true for leaders employed by the church, it is certainly true for lay leaders. One will probably never get rich or famous working for the Lord.

Martin Luther King, Jr. said, "Everyone has the opportunity for greatness—not for fame, but for greatness because greatness is determined by service."

The story is told of an old missionary couple on a ship coming home from years in self-sacrificing service. On the same ship was the president Theodore Roosevelt. When the ship docked, the president was met by a large crowd with great pomp and ceremony. But the old couple didn't have even one person to meet them. After getting their few belongings, they went and rented a humble apartment. By now the husband was feeling a little sad. "After all we have done, after all those years of service, we come home . . . but the president who just came home from a trip . . ." When his wife realized what her husband was thinking, she said, "Go talk to the Lord about it." He did, and soon he had a noticeably better attitude. "What did the Lord say," she wanted to know.

"He said we weren't home yet!" her husband replied.

The pay isn't always that great for being one of God's leaders, but remember we aren't home yet!

6. Leaders have always faced criticism.

"A critic is one who leaves no turn unstoned" wrote George Bernard Shaw. And unfortunately the church has more than its share of critics. Realistically, there always have been critics, and there always will be. The only way to avoid all criticism is to do nothing—and then you'll be criticized for being lazy!

Abraham Lincoln once said, "If I tried to read, much less answer, all the criticism made of me and all of the attacks leveled against me, this office would be closed for all other business. I do the best I know how, the very best I can, and I mean to keep on doing this down to the very end. If the end brings me out all wrong, ten angels swearing I had been right would make no difference. If the end brings me out all right, then what is said against me now will not amount to anything."

So take some consolation that you're not alone. Unfortunately there are those who feel it is their God-given responsibility to humble church leaders. But when we're the recipients of these occasional attacks, we need to keep them in proper perspective. Sacrifice has always been a part of leadership. William Miller, the dedicated and disciplined leader of the great awakening, faced incredible pressure and criticism. He once wrote:

My health is on the gain, as my folks would say. I have now only twenty-two boils from the bigness of a grape to a walnut, on my shoulder, side, back, and arms. I am truly afflicted like Job. And about as many comforters— only they do not come to see me as did Job's, and their arguments are not near so rational (Letter, May 3, 1843, quoted in *Signs of the Times,* May 17, 1843). That's commitment.

And on a significantly more serious note are the trials of some of our predecessors. The Council of Nicea in A.D. 325 was a turning point for the early Christian church. This significant church meeting followed the Roman persecution of A.D. 303–313, which was particularly aimed at the church leaders. History records the terrible scene. Diocletion and Galerius conducted the most bitter campaign of annihilation the Christians had ever suffered at the hand of Rome. They concentrated their terrorism on the ministers, thinking that if the shepherds were destroyed, the flocks would scatter. History records that when the ministers gathered some years later after the Council of Nicea in A.D. 325, they came— some without eyes, with arms torn from sockets, maimed in horrible ways. And these, as unbelievable as it may sound, were the fortunate ones!

I'm reminded of what inspiration says about our Leader, Christ. "They misinterpreted His words, falsified His statements, and impugned His motives" (Ellen G. White, *The Desire of Ages,* p. 392). The context for this statement was the crisis in Galilee. Many of Christ's followers had turned from Him, prompting Jesus to ask His disciples, "Are you going to leave Me, also?"

The obvious question that we must ask ourselves is this: If He, the perfect Leader, was so maligned, do we deserve better?

Ellen White makes the point that Jesus intentionally allowed the incident in Galilee to happen because if the disciples had not had their faith strengthened, then when the final crisis came they would not have been strong enough to endure. That's what Paul meant when he said:

> We are hard pressed on every side, but not crushed; per-plexed, but not in despair; persecuted, but not abandoned; struck down, but not destroyed. We always carry around in our body the death of Jesus, so that the life of Jesus may also be revealed in our body (2 Corinthians 4:8-10, NIV).

I'm realizing, more and more, that for the Christian, this life is a spiritual journey, not an arrival. It is a process, not a result. And what we often mistakenly see as an unpleasant event, God sees as just part of a process!

Once we come to grips with the reality that we will inevitably receive abuse as leaders for Him, our reaction to that can become tempered and even Christlike.

If sanctification is indeed the work of a lifetime, and if our lifetimes will be shortened due to the impending second coming of Christ, then we may be, in fact, on a time warp with an inordinate amount of growth needing to occur in a short period of time. Therefore, God's true leaders always have, and always will, receive criticism. Possibly it will be even more intense for us in the twenty-first century since we are indeed living in the last days.

If we had a magic wand we could wipe out all criticism, but that won't happen. And maybe in light of the above, it shouldn't. It may even get worse before it gets better, so we'd better get accustomed to it.

So like the commercial for Timex watches—one of the most trustworthy brands ever made—our slogan should be, "After the lickin'. . . we're still tickin'!" And remember, the retirement will be out of this world!

"It isn't the incompetent who destroy an organization.
The incompetent never get in a position to destroy it.
It is those who have achieved something and wish to rest upon
their achievements who are forever clogging things up."
—*Bits and Pieces.*

"Government by consensus is not leadership; it is fellowship,
designed to produce outcomes not that are right,
but that most people will support. The problem is that
sometimes the right decision is the least popular."
—*Richard Nixon.*

CHAPTER 10

DANCING ON PEANUT BUTTER

Peter Benchley wrote the best-selling novel *Jaws,* which subsequently became a popular Hollywood movie. He tells that before writing the book he went to Australia to observe sharks so as to become an expert. One day he waded out into the ocean, watching intently for sharks. Then Benchly saw a shark swimming toward him. He began running, as best he could, toward shore in the chest-high water. Later, when he had finally reached shore, he said he had "felt like he had been dancing on peanut butter."

Have you ever felt like that? Be honest. Have you ever felt that you were only going through the motions? Maybe even exerting some high energy output, only to be seemingly fruitless?

Your organization's statistics may even look quite good, at least compared to those of other organizations. But down deep you know you've lost your first love—the excitement, that drive to excel in ministry and soul winning. It's no longer there. You feel like you're just dancing on peanut butter.

Helen Keller was once asked, "Is there anything worse than being blind?" To which she gave a classic reply, "Oh, yes! A person with sight and no vision."

I'm being challenged right now by the text, "To whom much is given, from him much will be required" (Luke 12:48, NKJV). That must ever immunize us against the poison of complacency.

When we've lost our vision of who we are and where we are and why we're where we are, we can no longer be effective. We must not be so lulled by the poison of complacency that we forget we're in a cosmic battle and a great controversy.

Best-selling author Max Lucado put it this way:

> Pilgrims with no vision of the promised land became proprietors of their own land. Instead of looking upward at the Lord, they look inward at themselves and outward at each other. The result: cabin fever. Quarreling families (and church families). Restless leaders. Fence building. Staked off territory—No Trespassing signs are hung on hearts and homes.

Much of what has been said so far in this chapter could qualify as merely a form of sanctified motivational talk. But I want it to be more than that. We church leaders have a different motivation than that which drives the secular world. And we had better keep it focused and strong. It's no longer sufficient to compare ourselves with one another. "At that time I will search Jerusalem with lamps and punish those who are complacent . . . who think, 'the Lord will do nothing, either good or bad' " (Zephaniah 1:12, NIV).

WHEN GOOD THINGS HAPPEN TO GOOD PEOPLE

We've all read books and maybe even preached a sermon on "When bad things happen to good people." But have you ever thought about the flip side?—When good things happen to good people? Think about it. It's scary. There are many spiritual wreckages strewn along the road to success.

And there are likewise the wreckages of many leaders' families that God has blessed—to the point that they have lost their focus, lessened their dependence on Him, and eventually begun dancing on peanut butter, if not worse.

During the American Civil War, soldiers were sentenced to death for treason—sometimes even for falling asleep while standing guard. President Abraham Lincoln had a soft heart and occasionally would commute the sentence much to the consternation of his army commanders. On one occasion a young soldier was sentenced to hang for treason, and Lincoln was visited by the boy's distraught mother. Lincoln's parental heart was touched, and he pardoned the soldier. He then purportedly told the mother, "I still wish we could teach him a lesson. I wish we could give him a little bit of hanging."

Maybe we should pray, "Lord, give us a little bit of a hanging. Keep us from dancing on peanut butter. Keep us from the poison of complacency."

Now maybe I've gone from preaching to meddling, but human nature is really like the gravitational pull—as soon as we start going up, we tend to slide back down.

And all of us as leaders have to fight that dynamic. It's systemic. I'm supportive of our remuneration plan for the church. But the downside is that it doesn't take too much intelligence or too many years to figure something out. If my church baptizes seventy-five persons a year or ten, I get the same salary. If my school has a 50 percent enrollment increase or loses 5 percent, my monthly check stays the same. If I spend the morning working in my garden instead of making hospital visits, my pay isn't docked. If I spend the afternoon playing around with my computer rather than giving Bible studies, it's still the same number of years till retirement. And if I critcize evangelists or I lead my church into a public evangelistic reaping series each year, I still keep my job.

Mike Reagan, son of former President Reagan, and a talk show host, said after a recent California earthquake, "I feel like God reached down and shook my house and gave me a wake-up call." Will it take a wake-up call like that for us as leaders? God is still in the business of making big things happen.

"But," says someone, "I have unique challenges in my field of labor." Big obstacles? You bet! We all have them. But the facts are that most of us tend to be slowed down more by the incessant sand in our shoes than the mountains in our way. You see the obstacles only when you take your eyes off the goal.

I've heard people say that if Jesus were coming tomorrow, they'd live the same way as they are now. Well, I know what they mean, but the facts are, I believe, they'd live differently. You read the historical accounts of those living in 1844 before the Great Disappointment, and they were focused, they were driven, they were sacrificial.

So I challenge you—let's do more, by God's grace, then we've ever done before. Let's prayerfully counteract the poison of complacency.

One of the greatest golfers of all time is Arnold Palmer. In every tournament he played he always had a gallery of people following him. In one particular game he was not doing real well. In fact he became a bit discouraged.

Then someone in the crowd hollered out, "Arnie, charge! You've been holding back. You can do it!"

Palmer thought, *He's right. I have been too tentative.*

He took out his club and hit a beautiful shot. Then he sank it for a birdie. By the time he got to the back nine he was closing in on the leaders. Then he heard the same voice from the crowd, "Hey, Arnie, you can do it!"

There's that voice again, he thought. *And he's right, I can do it.* Again he took his putter and sank the ball for a birdie.

That day Palmer came back from five strokes behind on the back nine to win the tournament. It was a remarkable comeback.

As he stood on the victory stand to receive the trophy and the winner's check, he heard the now-familiar voice holler out, "Way to go, Arnie. You did it. We knew you could!"

Palmer looked at the crowd. "That voice," he said. "Who is that?" A little hand went up. Palmer weaved his way through the crowd to the spectator. "Sir, I want to thank you," he said. "I've heard you all day. Those were things I knew, but . . . and if there is ever anything I can do for you, just let me know."

"Well, there is something you can do for me, Arnie," said the man. "I'm a golfer myself. One thing I've always dreamed of doing is playing you a round—one on one. My name is Charlie Boswell."

"Charles Boswell. I've never heard of you."

"I'm the international champion for blind golfers."

Palmer hadn't noticed it before. Charles had a cane, and he wore dark glasses to cover where his eyes should have been for he didn't have any eyes. They were blown out in combat when he had gone back to save two people's lives. Subsequently he had been awarded the U.S. Congressional Medal of Honor for bravery. He was truly an inspiration to many.

And Arnold Palmer met him for the first time that day. "I would be honored to play a round of golf with you, Palmer told him."

Boswell said, "But I want your best shot—$1,000 or we don't play at all."

Now what do you do if you're Palmer? You don't want to take advantage of the guy, but you don't want to embarrass him either.

Arnold Palmer said, "OK, Charles. You're on! We'll play for $1,000. When do you want to play?"

And Charlie grinned and said, "Any night, Arnie; any night!"

Charlie had lost his sight, but he had never lost his vision!

I'm here to tell you like the voice from the crowd, "We can do it," by God's grace. As leaders, let's break the gravitational pull to mediocrity. Let's counteract the poison of complacency. Let's stop dancing on peanut butter.